COMMUNITY

COMMUNITY

The Structure of Belonging

PETER BLOCK

Second Edition
Revised and Updated

BK

Berrett–Koehler Publishers, Inc.
a BK Business book

Berrett-Koehler Publishers, Inc.
1333 Broadway, Suite 1000   Oakland, CA 94612-1921
Tel: (510) 817-2277   Fax: (510) 817-2278   www.bkconnection.com

ORDERING INFORMATION
Quantity sales. Special discounts are available on quantity purchases by corporations, associations, and others. For details, contact the "Special Sales Department" at the Berrett-Koehler address above.
Individual sales. Berrett-Koehler publications are available through most bookstores. They can also be ordered directly from Berrett-Koehler:
Tel: (800) 929-2929; Fax: (802) 864-7626; www.bkconnection.com.
Orders for college textbook / course adoption use. Please contact Berrett-Koehler: Tel: (800) 929-2929; Fax: (802) 864-7626.

Distributed to the U.S. trade and internationally by Penguin Random House Publisher Services.

Berrett-Koehler and the BK logo are registered trademarks of Berrett-Koehler Publishers, Inc.

Printed in the United States of America

Berrett-Koehler books are printed on long-lasting acid-free paper. When it is available, we choose paper that has been manufactured by environmentally responsible processes. These may include using trees grown in sustainable forests, incorporating recycled paper, minimizing chlorine in bleaching, or recycling the energy produced at the paper mill.

Library of Congress Cataloging-in-Publication Data

Names: Block, Peter, author.
Title: Community : the structure of belonging / Peter Block.
Description: Second Edition. I Oakland : Berrett-Koehler Publishers, 2018. I
      Revised edition of the author's Community, c2008.
Identifiers: LCCN 2018003687 I ISBN 9781523095568 (paperback)
Subjects: LCSH: Communities. I BISAC: BUSINESS & ECONOMICS / Organizational
      Behavior. I SOCIAL SCIENCE / Sociology / General. I SOCIAL SCIENCE / Customs & Traditions.
Classification: LCC HM756 .B56 2018 I DDC 307—dc23
LC record available at https://lccn.loc.gov/2018003687

SECOND EDITION

25 24 23 22 21 20   10 9 8 7 6 5 4 3

Developmental editor: Leslie Stephen
Copyeditor: Michele Jones
Book producer and text designer: Leigh McLellan Design
Cover designer: Bookwrights/Mayapriya Long
Indexer: Rachel Rice

To Maggie

In appreciation for your commitment, intelligence, love, and integrity that make what I do possible. You are a placeholder for all who give their talents and love in support of others. Your question "Who will do what by when?" changes the world.

Contents

The first human who hurled an insult
instead of a stone
was the founder of civilization.

Sigmund Freud

Welcome

This book is written to support those who care for the well-being of their community. It is for anyone who wants to be part of creating an organization, neighborhood, city, or country that works for all, and who has the faith and the energy to create such a place.

I am one of those people. Whenever I am in a neighborhood or small town and see empty storefronts, watch people floating aimlessly on the sidewalks during school or working hours, visit somewhere that seems like a hard place to raise a child or grow old, I am distressed and anguished. It has become impossible for me to ignore the fact that the world we are creating does not work well for all and increasingly does not work for most.

Along with this distress comes the knowledge that each of us, myself included, is participating in creating this world. If it is true that we are creating this world, then each of us has the power to heal its woundedness. This is not about guilt; it is about accountability. Citizens, in our capacity to come together and choose to be accountable, are our best shot at making a difference. This is true whether you want to improve conditions inside an organization or advance a cause or profession that you believe in, or are engaged in making your neighborhood or city a better place for all who live there.

To act on whatever our intentions might be to make the world better requires something more than individual action. It requires, in almost every case, people who may have little connection with each other, or who may even be on opposite sides of a question, to decide to come together for some common good. The need and the methodology to make this happen simply and quickly are what this book is about.

This truth has become clear in the wide range of unexpected invitations I have received since the book was originally published in 2006. I have been invited to a water scarcity conference in Calgary, Canada. I know nothing about water conservation; in fact, I am one of those people who leaves the water running while brushing my teeth. Companies have asked for help in building a community of mothers who purchase a certain diaper for their children. Ken Jaray was running for mayor of Manitou Springs and wanted to talk about using the community ideas both to run a campaign and to govern when elected. The faith community has repeatedly invited me into a discussion of ways to bring people together to begin a church where none exists and to explore ways to help existing churches more fully engage in the community and not rely on people finding meaning inside the church building. A university concerned about the safety of its students used the community-building ideas to engage its neighbors in taking collective action to make the neighborhood safer. Some cities, such as Colorado Springs, Colorado, even had several hundred groups use this book for their citywide book club with the intent of building a more connected community.

This tells me that the need for the experience of community, which is the collective capacity of citizens to make a difference, has only intensified. Even with all the means available to connect with each other, we live and function in ways that keep us isolated. Without new ways to come together, this isolation will persist.

Whatever it is you care about, to make the difference that you seek requires a group of people to learn to trust each other and choose to cooperate for a larger purpose.

The Second Edition

Steve Piersanti, my friend and publisher, called to suggest we put out another edition of this book. These invitations always make me nervous. I get nervous because I wonder if I have anything significant to add. After going through the book again, I chose to create another edition for three reasons. First, with nine years' experience putting its ideas into practice in my home city of Cincinnati, I can be clearer in expressing them. I have put more emphasis on what works, and extracted those thoughts that were nice, but had no durability. The fresh focus in this edition includes updating prior examples and adding a few new ones.

Second, there is growing interest in building community. Call it culture change in organizations, civic engagement in government, neighborhood building in the social sector, outreach in religion, or democracy in the larger society, there seems to be more and more awareness of the need to create places of belonging.

The third reason for developing a new edition is just my frustration and pain in seeing what is occurring in the world. Community building now seems to be an idea whose time has come. Its promise, though, is not well implemented. We still do a poor job of bringing people together. At best we convene a social event, a block party, or a reception, with food and music. All good things to do, but people most often huddle with like-minded people, and strangers remain strangers.

In the midst of the growing awareness of and innovation in thinking about the *need* to build community, the dominant practices for *how* to engage people, civically and organizationally, remain essentially unchanged. We still hold town meetings where one person talks and the rest ask vetted questions. City councils still sit on a platform with microphones and give citizens two minutes each to make their point. Too many gatherings still use PowerPoints for clarity and efficiency. Professional conferences continue to be designed around inspiring keynote speeches and content-filled workshops to attract attendees. Presenting data in this way becomes a weak substitute for learning and education.

Here is one example where the intention was mismatched with the design of the engagement process: In the face of growing poverty, a major city brought together the leaders from business, city government, social service institutions, and neighborhoods to form a task force to reduce poverty. The issue could have been any concern anywhere: education, health, safety, economic growth. In this case it was poverty. Great intention.

The strategy, however, was to follow the same predictable process that has not worked time and time again: First, a high-level steering committee was formed. Next, a sizeable amount of money was committed. Third, an expert outside research group was paid to analyze the problem. The group's findings were predictable: poverty is indeed a problem. This then led to setting bold goals and creating blueprints for actions, with timetables, milestones, and measures. This classic problem-solving approach basically called for trying harder at all the things that had been done for years. More mentoring of youth, better school achievement, more job training, greater commitment of large companies to hire more people from poverty neighborhoods. All useful, but nothing in the process raised awareness that poverty is basically a problem of economic isolation. Poverty is not just about the money; it is about the absence of possibility due to our isolation across economic classes, between elite and marginalized neighborhoods, between schools and their neighborhoods, between the elderly and young people. If this isolation, which is the breakdown of community, does not hold center stage, then nothing important will shift. Well-intentioned leaders and citizens, without the consciousness and the tools to produce authentic community, will simply be left with more programs, more funding, and eventually another study to analyze progress.

The option, with respect to poverty, is to realize that people living in economic isolation have skills, wisdom, capacities, and productive entrepreneurial energy. They have assets we don't see when we view them as problems to be analyzed, measured, and fixed. They don't need more schooling, services, and programs. They need access and relatedness to the wider community. They need to be seen as citizens worthy of investment capital and loans. They need partnerships with people and institutions across class and geographical boundaries. They require real partnerships, not mentors. There must be relatedness and trust where both sides give and receive. Building this kind of community is central to a strategy to create conditions where real transformation occurs. This is what is working in a few special places. This is the point being made in this book.

Shifting this consciousness and clarifying the tools are what this revised edition is about. To summarize, the following is what I have tried to emphasize in this edition:

Isolation is on the rise. This book is about the reconciliation or restoration of the experience of community. It offers ways of thinking and practice to return to a sense of belonging that this mobile, modernist, novelty-seeking culture lacks. It is clear that the isolation in our institutions, cities, and larger world seems to be increasing rather than decreasing. The extremism and rigid ideology that flood all forms of public conversation are painful to witness and, to my mind, partial determinants of the violence that surrounds us. Although social media promises to connect us, we still sit in Starbucks, walk down the street, and dine together staring at a flat screen. To restore our connectedness, we need to see clearly the isolation we are part of and to not be taken in by the myth of communal progress.

Interest and practice in restoring community are increasing. This trend goes under the name of civic engagement, community building, organizational outreach, community relations, democracy projects, cooperative movements—all caring for the well-being of the whole. A small example of interest in engagement is that communities and organizations have been selecting *Community* to share in local book clubs.

Institutional awareness of the need for community is growing. The not-so-obvious insight is that restoring community is increasingly seen as a productive strategy to address business and civic concerns. What is important, and new, is that our traditional institutions, such as the church, are moving their attention and faith efforts outside their buildings and into their neighborhoods. Places of congregation are now in taverns, common houses, and storefronts.

Rabbis and pastors are leading the community-building movement in forms such as the Parish Collective based in Seattle and the Hive and Just Love in Cincinnati.

The city government of Edmonton, Alberta, Canada, is sponsoring an Abundant Community Initiative, which supports neighbors in identifying and gathering together the gifts of people on their block in projects aimed at producing more safety and revitalization.

The Rochester Health Foundation has an eight-year strategy to reduce major illnesses in the community by organizing residents in vulnerable neighborhoods to make their place better, addressing concerns that would seem to have nothing to do with major diseases. They are investing in such projects as beautification, community gardens, fixing up distressed buildings, and pushing drug traffic out. What does having residents care for their six-block area have to do with fighting cancer, diabetes, and heart disease? There is evidence that some of the major determinants of disease are social, relational, and communal.

When we have serious structural innovation in community engagement on the part of the church, the government, and foundations, something important is going on.

One more motivation for revising the book is to confront the reality that even when social pioneers do amazing work and manage to bring people together to make a place better, their work remains an untold story. It competes poorly for all the attention drawn to crisis. Building trust, relationships, and social capital as a strategy for improving health, well-being, and safety and for raising productive children does not make a lot of money for anybody and does not feed the media's—social media included—appetite for drama and entertainment. What works in the world, as opposed to what is failing in the world, still gets treated as a human interest story.

All the more reason to keep clarifying why building community and belonging is going to be our most powerful strategy for ending the displacement and isolation that plagues so many aspects of our world. Building community is also a powerful strategy for creating resilient organizations, a healthier planet, and safer streets. The purpose of this book is to put the capacity to do this in the hands of citizens, supported, as a backup in the end, by the usual solutions of designing programs, making blueprints, getting funding, and trying all the things that institutions do.

The challenge in this enterprise is that building community seems too simple. If you choose to shift toward a context of possibility instead of staying with a context of deficiency, and you follow the questions and protocols outlined in part 2, you will discover how simple it is to end people's isolation. When you reduce people's isolation, they learn that they are not crazy and that there is nothing wrong with them. To this end, here is a preview of how I approached this edition:

- I have included more examples of how a shift to community building may be more powerful than traditional problem solving and programs. How we approach the persistence of the poverty scenario I describe here is one example. Interspersed throughout the text are more instances where social capital, the product of building community, is decisive in creating economic reform where it is most needed.

- In addition to amplifying the need for community and belonging, I show how really simple building community can be, once we decide it is essential. Overcoming isolation and creating belonging does not take a long time. Like yoga, it is about attention and practice and the mat you are on in the moment. It is not about the particular people and their agility or body shape, nor does it take years of effort. The structure of belonging is simply about getting the room right, forming small groups, getting the questions right, and putting a lid on our desire to rescue, fix, and train.

- I have repurposed the last part of the book to make it a more useful tool for readers to refresh their knowledge of key concepts, reflect on why these ideas are so elusive in our lives, and think about what they might mean if applied in everyday situations. I have also taken the long list of role models and resources out of the book and placed them on the abundantcommunity.com website.

The Importance of Belonging

In making all these changes, I have accentuated the major point of the book: that the strong cultural imperative of individualism and the belief that science and technology will solve the problems of climate, corporate productivity, school performance, customer satisfaction, and immortality will only increase the violence, poverty, and unnecessary suffering that we are confronted with every day. Community and its structure of belonging does something about this.

The word *belong* has two meanings. First and foremost, to belong is to be related to and a part of something. It is membership, the experience of being at home in the broadest sense of the phrase. Belonging is best created when we join with other people in producing something that makes a place better. It is the opposite of thinking *I must do it on my own*. That wherever I am, it is all on my shoulders and that perhaps I would be better off somewhere else. The opposite of belonging is to feel isolated and always (all ways) on the margin, an outsider. I am still forever wandering, looking for that place where I belong. To belong is to know, even in the middle of the night, that I am among friends.

Our purpose in exploring the concepts and methods of community building is to increase the amount of belonging or relatedness that exists in the world. We do this partly out of a desire for good, but primarily because if we want to fill those empty storefronts, raise our children, and engage those wandering on the sidewalks during the day, building community is a precondition for those changes to occur. Experiencing the kind of friendship, hospitality, and conviviality that constitutes community is not easy or natural in the world we now live in, and that is why the storefronts stay empty, the children stay challenged, and suffering stays around us.

The second meaning of the word *belong* has to do with being an owner: something belongs to me. To belong to a community is to act as a creator and co-owner of that community. What I consider mine I will build and nurture. The work, then, is to seek in our communities a wider and deeper sense of emotional ownership and communal ownership. It means fostering among all of a community's citizens a sense of ownership and accountability, both in their relationships and in what they actually control.

Belonging can also be thought of as a longing to be. Being is our capacity to find our deeper purpose in all that we do. It is the capacity to be present and to discover our authenticity and whole selves. This is often thought of as an individual capacity, but it is also a community capacity. Community is the container within which our longing to be is fulfilled. Without the connectedness of a community, we will continue to choose not to be. I have always been touched by the term *beloved community*. This is often expressed in a spiritual context, but it also is possible in the secular aspects of our everyday life.

My intent in this book is to give definition to ways of structuring the experience of belonging—that's why the first noun in its subtitle is *structure*. Belonging does not have to be left to chance or to be dependent on the welcoming nature of others.

My thinking about structure has been shaped by a quote from a wonderful periodical devoted to art and architecture called *The Structurist*:

> The word *structure* means to build, to construct, to form, as well as the organization or morphology of the elements involved in the process. It can be seen as the embodiment of creation . . . a quest not only for form but also for purpose, direction and continuity.

This quote refers to art, and we can apply the same thoughts to community. The promise of what follows in this book is to provide structural ways to create the experience of belonging, not only in places where people come just to be together socially but especially in places where we least expect it. These include all the places where people come together to get something done—our meetings, dialogues, conferences, planning processes—all those gatherings where we assemble to reflect on and decide the kind of future we want for ourselves.

I especially like the word *structure* because it stands in relief to our concern about style. To offer structures with the promise of creating community gives leaders relief from the common story that leadership is a set of personal qualities we are born with, develop, or try on like a new suit to see if they fit. The structures in this book—both the thinking and the practices—can be chosen and implemented regardless of personal style, or lack thereof. We can create structures of belonging even if we are introverted and do not like to make eye contact.

A word about the structure of the book. I have included a summary of each chapter at its beginning. I got the idea from Christopher Alexander's *Timeless Way of Building*. There he said that if you do not want to read the whole book or a whole chapter, just read the summaries and you will get the point. Also, the main points are summarized in outline form at the end, so if you do not want to read the chapter summaries or the text, you can go to the last section of the book and really save some time.

The Fragmented Community and Its Transformation

The essential challenge is to transform the isolation and self-interest within our communities into connectedness and caring for the whole. The key is to identify how this transformation occurs. We begin by shifting our attention from the problems of community to the possibility of community. We also need to acknowledge that our wisdom about individual transformation is not enough when it comes to community transformation. The purpose here is to bring together our knowledge about the nature of collective transformation. A key insight in this pursuit is to accept the importance of social capital to the life of the community. This begins the effort to create a future distinct from the past.

• • •

The need to create a structure of belonging grows out of the isolated nature of our lives, our institutions, and our communities. The absence of belonging is so widespread that we might say we are living in an age of isolation, imitating the lament from early in the last century, when life was referred to as the age of anxiety. Ironically, we talk today of how small our world has become, with the shrinking effect of globalization, instant sharing of information, quick technology, and workplaces that operate around the globe.

Our world is organized around certain principles that are marketed as if they produce community, but their effects are the opposite. Here are a few:

Convenience: In earlier days, we were promised leisure time with the invention of the dishwasher, washing machine, and our own telephone line. Now we shop online, have gourmet ready-to-cook or already-cooked meals delivered to our home, speak into a device that saves our shopping list and then places the order with the grocery store for us to pick up in our car or have delivered to our home. And for a slight upcharge, the grocer will put our groceries away in our kitchen.

Speed: Speed in and of itself has become a value. Faster is better. Wait time on the phone is intolerable, so now we get automated responses, called bots. In fact, in the world of commerce, we are reaching the point where we would rather talk to an intelligent machine than to a human being. We also seem more pressed for time, valuing all things virtual.

Electronic connections: Texts, emails, Instagram, Twitter, and more make constant sharing of images and information easy and entertaining. They promise to give us more time and increased productivity; better networks are sold as a connected world.

Yet there is the question of whether any of these examples produce the sense of community and belonging that reduces our isolation and produces well-being. These developments provide contact, diverse information, an infinite range of opinion. But they do not create the connection from which we can become grounded and experience the sense of safety that arises from a place where we are emotionally, spiritually, and psychologically a member.

In addition to the changing features of modern culture, our isolation occurs because Western culture, our individualistic narrative, the inward attention of our institutions and our professions, and the messages from our media all serve to fragment us. We are broken into pieces.

One aspect of our fragmentation is the gaps between sectors of our cities and neighborhoods; businesses, schools, social service organizations, churches, and government operate mostly in their own worlds. Each piece is working hard on its own purpose, but parallel effort added together does not make a community. Our communities are separated into silos; they are a collection of institutions and programs operating near one another but not overlapping or touching. This is important to understand because it is this dividedness that makes it so difficult to create a more positive or alternative future—especially in a culture that is much more interested in individuality and independence than in interdependence. The challenge in creating a place that works for all—for youth, people with disabilities, people economically or socially isolated—is our need for a way to overcome these inherent cultural forces. This calls for a shift in narrative which says that individualism, risk, and competition are just *one story* of who we are; they are not *the story* of who we are. Our work is to shift the narrative by designing ways of coming together that become an example of the future we desire.

Creating the sense that we are safe and among friends, especially those we have not yet met, is a particular challenge for our cities and rural towns. The dominant narrative about our cities is that they are unsafe and troubled. Those we label "homeless" or "ex-offenders" or "disabled" or "at risk" are the most visible people who struggle with belonging, but isolation and apartness is also a wider condition of modern life. This is as true in our gated communities and suburbs as in our urban centers.

There is a particular isolation in the spaciousness and comfort of our suburbs. In these neighborhoods, we needed to invent the "play date" for our children. Interaction among kids must be scheduled, much like a business meeting. On Tuesday, a mom must call another mom and ask, "Can Alex play with Phil on Thursday, at our house, say about four o'clock? I'll call if we're running late. The play date should last until roughly 5:45, to give both children time to freshen up for the family get-together at dinner." A far cry from the days when kids walked home after school and casually played with whomever they ran into.

The cost of our detachment and disconnection is not only our isolation, our loneliness, but also that there are too many people in our communities whose gifts remain on the margin. Filling the need for belonging is not just a personal struggle for connection but also a community problem, which is our primary concern in this book. We have a hundred ways of encouraging individual development, but we are semiliterate when it comes to the question of communal development. We rarely act on the insight that the way we gather, and the nature of our conversation about who we are as a collective, shift the context toward the circle and away from the pyramid as a symbol of our way of organizing ourselves. The effects of the fragmentation of our communities show up in low voter turnout, the struggle to sustain volunteerism, and the large portion of the population who remain disengaged.

The struggle is also the reality for the millions of people around the world who are part of today's diaspora—the growing number of displaced people unable to return to their homeland, living and raising their children in a permanent state of transition.

Our isolation is as much an act of imagination as it is the reality of our experience. The Jews were slaves in ancient Egypt for four hundred years. Until the end, they participated in their slavery by thinking it was their destiny. Once they cried out and imagined they could be free, an alternative was put in motion. Our isolation is a modern form of slavery—a limitation, to state it more gently. The moment we realize how isolated we are, and that this isolation is not inevitable, then creating a community that ends unnecessary suffering becomes a possibility. If we stay in isolation, we will always blame ourselves and each other to explain our condition. We will stay focused on our limits, on what we lack, on our need for more money, more training, more of everything. Real change will carry the same odds as a lottery ticket.

Communities That Work for All

Community offers the promise of belonging and calls for us to acknowledge our interdependence. To belong is to act as an investor, owner, and creator of this place. To be welcome, even if we are strangers. As if we came to the right place and are affirmed for that choice.

To feel a sense of belonging is important because it will lead us from conversations about safety and comfort to other conversations, such as those about our relatedness and willingness to provide hospitality and generosity. Hospitality is the welcoming of strangers, and generosity is extending an offer with no expectation of return. These are two elements that we want to nurture as we work to create, strengthen, and restore our communities. This will not occur in a culture dominated by isolation and its correlate, fear.

•   •   •

In a book like this there is always the temptation to provide proof and examples of what healthy communities look like and where they exist. This is called benchmarking. There are great teams in every organization, great neighborhoods in every city, and great cities in every country. There are some examples on the abundantcommunity.com website. They give us hope and possibility. When seen as benchmarks, they make for good journalism, but benchmarking has an element of illusion built in. It implies that if I can see it there, I can create it here. The hard part of building community is that it is always a custom job. It is born of local people, with unique gifts, deciding what to create together in this place.

The intent here is to explore the concepts and tools to create the custom job of producing authentic community. How is community transformed? What fundamental shifts are involved? Too little is understood about the creation and transformation of a collective. I want to explore a way of thinking that creates an opening for authentic communities to exist and details what each of us can do to make that happen. The essence is to take a step forward in our thinking about the importance of having citizens connect with each other. The moment we decide this is essential, then we can be specific about ways to redesign every meeting, gathering, civic event so that this idea of citizens connecting, face-to-face, with each other can be put into practice. This creates the condition where people in communities can come together to produce something new for themselves. By thinking in terms of a structure of belonging, we begin to build the capacity to transform our communities into ones that work for all.

The challenge is to think broadly enough to have a theory and a methodology that have the power to make a difference, yet are simple and clear enough to be accessible to anyone who wants to make that difference. We need ideas from a variety of places and disciplines to deal with the complexity of community. Then, acting as if these ideas are true, we must translate them into embarrassingly simple and concrete acts.

This means a shift in thinking that gives us clues about collective possibility. The shift in thinking is the focus of chapters 1 through 7. Following that, we come to methodology, which many of you may consider the heart of the book. But without the shift in thinking, methodology becomes technique, and practice becomes imitation.

· · ·

One key perspective is that to create a more positive and connected future for our communities, we must be willing to trade their problems for their possibilities. This trade is what is necessary to create a future for our cities and neighborhoods, organizations and institutions—a future that is distinct from the past. Which is the point.

To create an alternative future, we need to advance our understanding of the nature of communal or collective transformation. We know a good deal about individual transformation, but our understanding of the transformation of human systems, such as our workplaces, neighborhoods, and towns, is primitive at best, and too often naïve in the belief that if enough individuals are trained and become more intentional and compassionate human beings, a shift in the culture of a community or institution will occur. Collective transformation does not happen this way.

A Future Distinct from the Past

The core question, then, is this: What is the means through which those of us who care about the whole community can create a future for ourselves that is not just an improvement but one of a different nature from what we now have?

This is why we are not focused on individual transformation in this book. Individual transformation is the more popular conversation, and the choice not to focus on it is because we have already learned that the transformation of large numbers of individuals does not result in the transformation of communities. If we continue to invest in individuals as the primary target of change, we will spend our primary energy on this and never fully invest in communities. In this way, individual transformation comes at the cost of community.

• • •

The fact that a sense of community has practical importance is probably best established in the work of Robert Putnam in his book *Bowling Alone.* He found that individual health, educational achievement, local economic strength, and other measures of community well-being were dependent on the level of *social capital* that exists in a community.

Geography, history, great leadership, fine programs, economic advantage, or any other factors that we traditionally use to explain success made only a marginal difference in the health, education, or economic strength of a community. A community's well-being simply had to do with the quality of the relationships, the cohesion that exists among its citizens. Putnam calls this *social capital.*

Social capital is about acting on and valuing our interdependence and sense of belonging. It is measured by how much we trust each other and how much we cooperate to make a place better. It is the extent to which we extend hospitality and affection to one another. If Putnam is right, to improve the common measures of community health—economy, education, health, safety, the environment—we need to create a community where each citizen has the experience of being connected to those around them and knows that their safety and success are dependent on the success of all others.

This is an important insight for our cities. If you look beneath the surface of even our finest cities and neighborhoods, there is too much suffering. It took the broken levees of Hurricane Katrina to expose to the world the poverty and fragile lives in New Orleans. Poverty continues to worsen, even in times of seeming economic growth. Drug addiction remains immune to all the wars against it.

Community Now

I live in Cincinnati, Ohio, which like most of our urban centers has both abundant, irreplaceable qualities and assets, and also challenges that are impossible to ignore, try as we might. Wherever we live, we are never more than a short ride from neighborhoods that are wounded with disabled buildings and people working hard to barely get by. In this culture, we marginalize these neighbors. To not see the struggle of those on the margin, to think this is the best of all possible worlds or that we are doing fine, especially if our particular street or neighborhood is safe and prosperous, is to live with blinders on.

We choose to live with blinders for good reason. There is great attraction to the suburban life, the upscale urban and rural life, and the dream of residing in "hot" places. We are constantly reminded of the allure of gated communities, quaint and prosperous small towns, nationally acclaimed golden cities. The streets we most frequently hear about in these areas are clean and busy with pedestrians, their housing a string of jewels, the center city vital and alive, and neighborhoods the source of great pride.

These prosperous places, though, are only the partial story. Take it from Jim Keene, a very wise and successful public servant. He has brought his humanity and vision into the cauldron of building community as city manager for Berkeley, Tucson, and now Palo Alto, California. Jim once said that for every city that prospers, there is another city nearby that is paying the price for that prosperity.

We know we have a shrinking middle class, a growing separation between the well off and the underclass. You cannot look closely at even the great cities in the world without seeing serious underemployment, poverty, homelessness, neighborhoods with empty buildings, a deteriorating environment, youth hanging out on street corners day and night, and concerns about public safety.

We know about the dropout rates and deplorable conditions of our urban schools and the difficulty of achieving affordable health care for all. The list goes on. But this is not the point. The question here is not about the nature of the struggles; it is about the nature of the cure. The belief here is that without the foundation of a connected community, these conditions will not improve, regardless of the money and programs we are constantly delivering.

So the focus in this book is about shifting these conditions in our communities, in both those places that are paying the price *and* their more prosperous neighbors. For even in prosperous places, the idea and experience of community are elusive. If you look closely, you realize that the social fabric of our culture is more fragile than we imagine.

PART ONE

The Fabric of Community

The social fabric of community is shaped by the idea that only when we are connected and care for the well-being of the whole is a civil and democratic society created. It is like the Bodhisattva belief that not one of us can enter Nirvana until all others have gone before us.

> What is extra-ordinary appears to us as a habit, the dawn a daily routine of nature.
>
> Abraham Joshua Heschel

What makes community building so complex is that it occurs in an infinite number of small steps, sometimes in quiet moments that we notice out of the corner of our eye. It calls for us to treat as important many things that we thought were incidental. An afterthought becomes the point; a comment made in passing defines who we are more than all that came before. If the artist is one who captures the nuance of experience, then this is who each of us must become. Seeing through the eyes of the artist reflects the intimate nature of community, even if it is occurring among large groups of people.

The key to creating or transforming community, then, is to see the power in the small but important elements of being with others. The shift we seek needs to be embodied in each invitation we make, each relationship we encounter, and each meeting we attend. For at the most operational and practical level, after all the thinking about policy, strategy, mission, and milestones, the structure of belonging gets down to this: How are we going to be when we gather together?

CHAPTER 1

Insights into Transformation

Social fabric is created one room at a time. It is formed from small steps that ask "Who do we want in the room?" and "What is the new conversation that we want to occur?" In community building, we choose the people and the conversation that will produce the accountability to build relatedness, structure belonging, and move the action forward. It is in this process that accountability is chosen and care for the well-being of the whole is embodied. Individual transformation is not the point; weaving and strengthening the fabric of community is a collective effort and starts from a shift in our mind-set about our connectedness.

A series of core insights informs us how to answer these questions. These insights include ideas about focusing on gifts, on associational life, and on the way all transformation occurs through language. Also critical are insights about the context that governs the conversations and the willingness to speak into the future.

Two additional strands in the fabric of community explored here are the need for each small step to capture a quality of aliveness and be an example of the larger world we want to inhabit. There is an established method for accomplishing this aliveness that values all voices in the room, uses the small group even in large gatherings, and recognizes that accountability grows out of the act of cocreation. The essence of creating an alternative future comes from citizen-to-citizen engagement that focuses at each step on the well-being of the whole.

● ● ●

M ajor influences on the belief system underlying this methodology of communal transformation come from several disciplines
and people whose work has been radical in many ways; their insights are
foundational for our purposes. There are many others who inform us and
are mentioned in this book, but these five touch the core: John McKnight,
Werner Erhard, Robert Putnam, Christopher Alexander, and Peter Koestenbaum. The sixth collection of insights is from a group of wizards who have
given life to large group methodologies—some of whom are Marvin Weisbord, Kathie Dannemiller, Dick and Emily Axelrod, Carolyn Lukensmeyer,
Barbara Bunker, Billie Alban, and David Isaacs and Juanita Brown.

There are two more people whose insights are important to understanding how the world changes. One is David Bornstein. His book *How
to Change the World* analyzes nine social entrepreneurs who created large
social movements around the globe. David's summary of why they were
successful is worth our attention. Finally, I too briefly include the thinking
of Allan Cohen. He translates the world of emergence and complex adaptive
systems into language that once in a while I begin to think I understand.

I chose all of these people because I personally know most of them, and
they are the ones who have shaken my own thinking; their ideas have, for
me, endured the test of time and experience.

What follows is a summary of the aspects of these people's work that
are useful to this enterprise. I'll summarize their insights briefly here and
then weave them throughout the rest of the book.

The McKnight Insights:
Gifts, Associational Life, and Power

John McKnight is a leading light in the world of understanding the nature
of community and what builds it. Three of his insights have permanently
changed my thinking.

Focus on gifts. First and foremost, he asserts that community is built
by focusing on people's gifts rather than their deficiencies. In the world of
community and volunteerism, deficiencies have no market value; gifts are

the point. Citizens in community want to know what you can do, not what you can't do.

In the professional world of service providers, whole industries have been built on people's deficiencies. Social services and most of medicine, therapy, and psychology are organized around what is missing or broken in people.

McKnight points out that if you go to a professional service provider and say you have no deficiencies or problems, that you just want to talk about your gifts and talents, you will be shown the door and treated as though you are wasting their time. Go to an association or a group of neighbors and tell them what your capabilities are, and they get quite interested.

This insight is profound if taken seriously, for it eliminates most of the conversations we now have about problem diagnosis, gap analysis (if you do not know what this is, be grateful), weaknesses, and what's wrong with me, you, and the rest of the world. It also underscores the limitation of labeling people. McKnight knows that the act of labeling, itself, is what diminishes the capacity of people to fulfill their potential. If we care about transformation, then we will stay focused on gifts, to such an extent that our work becomes simply to bring the gifts of those on the margin into the center.

John's focus on gifts has led to his founding a worldwide movement called Asset-Based Community Development. Simply put, this movement declares that if we want to make communities stronger, we should study their assets, resources, and talents. It is in the attention to these things that something new can occur.

Associational life. The second insight that is relevant here has to do with the limitations of systems. John sees a system as an organized group of funded and well-resourced professionals who operate in the domain of cases, clients, and services. As soon as you professionalize care, you have produced an oxymoron. He says that systems are capable of service but not care. Talk to any poor person or vulnerable person and they can give you a long list of the services they have received. They are well serviced, but you often have to ask what in their life has fundamentally changed.

The alternative to a system is what John calls "associational life": groups of people voluntarily coming together to do some good. In the disabilities world, John's work has been enthusiastically received. This has led to a widespread effort to take people with visible disabilities out of institutions and systems and bring them back into neighborhoods. Support groups are created, slowly, voluntarily, with a lot of phone calls and requests, so that ordinary citizens come together to support their new neighbors. This strategy brings generosity back into a neighborhood, and in the doing, citizens whose disabilities are hidden (all of us) experience a transformation in their own lives.

Power in our hands. The third insight for community building is John's faith in citizens to identify and solve problems for themselves. He finds that most sustainable improvements in community occur when citizens discover their own power to act. Whatever the symptom—drugs, deteriorating houses, poor economy, displacement, violence—it is when citizens stop waiting for professionals or elected leadership to do something, and decide they can reclaim what they have delegated to others, that things really happen. This act of power is present in most stories of lasting community improvement and change.

To summarize these insights from the work of John McKnight and his partner, Jody Kretzmann: Communities are built from the assets and gifts of their citizens, not from the citizens' needs or deficiencies. Organized, professionalized systems are capable of delivering services, but only associational life is capable of delivering care. Sustainable transformation is constructed in those places where citizens, not institutions or experts, choose to come together to produce a desired future.

The Erhard Insights:
The Power of Language, Context, and Possibility

For over thirty years, Werner Erhard has created thinking and learning experiences that have affected millions of people's lives. Many of the ideas he has worked with derive from the work of others, but Werner has named and integrated them into something more powerful than where the thinking began. His work lives through the Landmark Corporation and other licensees. What I select from his work here is a small part of his legacy, but these are the ideas that have changed my life and practice.

The power of language. Werner understands the primal creative nature of language. Many of us have focused for years on improving conversations. We have known that dialogue and communication are important tools for improvement. Werner takes it to a whole new realm by asserting that all transformation is linguistic.

He believes that a shift in speaking and listening is the essence of transformation. If we have any desire to create an alternative future, it is only going to happen through a shift in our language. If we want a change in culture, for example, the work is to change the conversation—or, more precisely, to have a conversation that we have not had before, one that has the power to create something new in the world. This insight forces us to question the value of our stories, the positions we take, our love of the past, and our way of being in the world.

The power of context. Another insight is in the statement, "The context is decisive." This means that the way we function is powerfully impacted by our worldview, or the way, in his language, that "the world shows up for us." Nothing in our doing or the way we go through life will shift until we can question, and then choose once again, the basic set of beliefs—some call it mental models; we're calling it context here—that lie behind our actions. Quoting Werner, "Contexts are constituted in language, so we do have something to say about the contexts that limit and shape our actions."

Implied in this insight is that we have a choice over the context within which we live. Plus, as an added bargain, we can choose a context that better suits who we are now without the usual requirements of years of inner work, a life-threatening crisis, finding a new relationship, or going back to school (the most common transformational technologies of choice).

The way this happens (made too simple here) is by changing our relationship with our past. We do this by realizing, through a process of reflection and rethinking, how we have not completed our past and unintentionally keep bringing it into the future. The shift happens when we pay close attention to the constraints of our listening and accept that our stories are our limitation. This ultimately creates an opening for a new future to occur.

The power of possibility. Changing our relationship with our past leads to another aspect of language that Werner has carefully developed. This is an understanding of the potential in the concept and use of *possibility*. *Possibility* as used here is distinguished from other words like *vision, goals, purpose,* and *destiny.* Each of those has its own profound meaning, but all are different from the way Werner uses the word *possibility.* Possibility, here, is a declaration: a declaration of what we create in the world each time we show up. It is a condition, or value, that we want to occur in the world, such as peace, inclusion, relatedness, or reconciliation. A possibility is brought into being in the act of declaring it.

For example: if you declare that you are the possibility of peace in the world, though peace may not reign at this moment, the possibility of peace enters the room just because you have walked in the door. Peace here is a future not dependent on achievement; it is a possibility. The possibility is created by our declaration, and then, thankfully, it begins to work on us. The breakthrough is that we become that possibility, and this is what is transforming. The catch is that possibility can work on us only when we have come to terms with our story. Whatever we hold as our story, which is our version of the past, and from which we take our identity, becomes the limitation to living into a new possibility.

Werner has described this with more precision in personal correspondence:

> I suggest that you consider making it clear that it is the future that one lives into that shapes one's being and action in the present. And, the reason that it appears that it is the past that shapes one's being and action in the present is that for most people the past lives in (shapes) their view of the future. . . .
>
> [I]t's only by completing the past (being complete with the past) such that it no longer shapes one's being and action in the present that there is room to create a new future (one not shaped by the past—a future that wasn't going to happen anyhow). Futures not shaped by the past (i.e., a future that wasn't going to happen anyhow) are constituted in language.

In summary, (1) one gets complete with the past, which takes it out of the future (being complete with the past is not to forget the past); (2) in the room that is now available in the future when one's being and action are no longer shaped by the past, one creates a future (a future that moves, touches, and inspires one); (3) that future starts to shape one's being and actions in the present so that they are consistent with realizing that future.

Werner Erhard's way of thinking about language, context, and possibility are key elements in any thinking about authentic transformation. As with the other insights here, they are about a way of being in the world first, and then they can be embodied in concrete actions.

The Putnam Insights:
Social Capital and the Well-Being of Community

Robert Putnam wrote *Bowling Alone* and amplified the conversation about the role that social capital plays in building community. As one part of his extensive research, he studied a fair number of Italian towns and tried to understand why some were more democratic, were more economically successful, had better health, and experienced better educational achievement.

His findings were startling, for he discovered that the one thing that distinguished the more successful from the less successful towns was the extent of social capital, or widespread relatedness that existed among its citizens. Success as a town was not dependent on the town's geography, history, economic base, cultural inheritance, or financial resources.

Putnam shows how we have become increasingly disconnected from family, friends, neighbors, and our democratic structures—and how we may reconnect. He warns that our stock of social capital—the very fabric of our connections with each other—has plummeted, impoverishing our lives and communities.

As earlier mentioned about Putnam, geography, history, great leadership, fine programs, economic advantage, and any other factors that we traditionally use to explain success made only a marginal difference in the health of a community. Community well-being simply had to do with the quality of the relationships, the cohesion that exists among its citizens. He calls this *social capital.*

In the book *Better Together,* Putnam and coauthor Lewis M. Feldstein explain that "*social capital* refers to social networks, norms of reciprocity, mutual assistance, and trustworthiness. The central insight of this approach is that social networks have real value both for the people in those networks . . . as well as for bystanders. Criminologists, for instance, have shown that the crime rate in a neighborhood is lowered when neighbors know one another well, benefiting even residents who are not themselves involved in neighborhood activities."

They go on to distinguish between "bonding" and "bridging" social capital. Bonding social capital comprises networks that are inward look-ing, composed of people of like mind. Other social networks "encompass different types of people and tend to be outward looking—bridging social capital." It is primarily the bridging social capital that we are interested in here. As Putnam and Feldstein put it: "a society that has *only* bonding social capital will . . . [be] segregated into mutually hostile camps. So a pluralistic democracy requires lots of bridging social capital, not just the bonding variety."

The Alexander Insights: Aliveness, Wholeness, and Unfolding

Christopher Alexander speaks from the world of architecture, but his think-ing applies equally well to the creation of community. He grieves over the fragmented and mechanistic way we currently operate. In *The Nature of Order: An Essay on the Art of Building and the Nature of the Universe, Book 1: The Phenomenon of Life,* he writes,

> In discussing what to do in a particular part of a town, one person
> thinks poverty is the most important thing. Another person thinks
> ecology is the most important thing. Another person takes traffic
> as his point of departure. Another person views the maximization
> of profit from development as the guiding factor. All these points of
> view are understood to be individual, legitimate, and inherently in

conflict. It is assumed that there is not a unitary view through which these many realities can be combined. They simply get slugged out in the marketplace, or in the public forum.

But instead of lucid insight, instead of growing communal awareness of what should be done in a building, or in a park, even on a tiny bench—in short, of what is good—the situation remains one in which several dissimilar and incompatible points of view are at war in some poorly understood balancing act.

Aliveness and wholeness. The alternative to this fragmentation is to create structures that are defined by what Alexander calls "a quality of aliveness." The absence or presence of this quality has profound impact on the experience of being in that structure. Also, for that quality of aliveness to be present in the final product, it must be present in each step in the design and creation of the structure.

This aliveness grows out of a sense of wholeness. Wholeness is made up of a collection of separate centers, where each center has "a certain life or intensity. . . . We can see that the life of any one center depends on the life of other centers. This life or intensity is not inherent in the center by itself, but is a function of the whole configuration in which the center occurs."

To connect this to our discussion, we must ask whether every single step in our work holds this quality of life or intensity. Whether we're talking about a strategy, program, invitation, dialogue, gathering, or the building of a master plan, the human experience of aliveness in each choice or step has as much significance as any technical, economic, or purely practical consideration.

This aliveness also is most often found in surprising places. Often in irregular structures, all with aspects of imperfection. Alexander identifies fifteen properties that create the wholeness and aliveness. It would take us off track to list them all here, but some are clearly to the point. Listen to the language he uses, and you get a feel for the world he is naming: Deep Interlock and Ambiguity, Contrast, Roughness, Simplicity and Inner Calm, Not-Separateness.

It is easy to take these words, which he uses to reflect qualities in nature and in a room or building, and apply them to the world of social capital, human relatedness, and belonging that we are concerned with here. Much of what follows in the book is just this: bringing aliveness and wholeness to our notions of leadership, citizenship, social structures, and context, which are essential in creating the community of belonging and restoration that we desire.

Transformation as unfolding. One more influence from Alexander is his belief that aliveness and wholeness can occur only through a process of "unfolding." Transformation unfolds and is given structure by a consciousness of the whole. The task of transformation is to operate so that what we create grows organically, more concerned with the "quality of aliveness" that gives us the experience of wholeness than with a predictable destination and the speed with which we can reach it.

An unfolding strategy requires giving an uncomfortable importance to each small step we take. We have to worry as much about the arrangement of a room as we do about the community issue that caused us to assemble. It leads us to value the details of each step so that each step becomes its own center. For example, each step of a master plan has to be a small example of the qualities we want in the final large thing. Throughout this book, you will see the effort to value the importance of small things; this intention is a direct outgrowth of Alexander's insights.

In summary, Christopher Alexander moves us toward aliveness, embodied in those places and moments that give us the experience of belonging. In the absence of aliveness, we unknowingly experience an inner conflict, a feeling of something unresolved.

The Koestenbaum Insights: Paradox, Freedom, and Accountability

For several decades, Peter Koestenbaum has brought the insights of philosophy to the business marketplace. His work on the Leadership Diamond paints a holistic and practical landscape of what is required of leaders to achieve greatness in the world, both personally and for their institutions.

Appreciating paradox. One insight that informs our exploration of communal transformation is Peter's understanding of how we can come to terms with the paradoxical nature of human affairs. He values ambiguity and anxiety as the natural condition of being human. The painful choices people make in their lives and for their institutions are an affirming aspect of their humanity. These choices are not the sign of a problem or weakness or the world gone wrong. It is out of the subjectivity and complexity of life that transformation emerges. As a philosopher and consultant, Peter has always given voice to how profound the right question can be.

It is the willingness to reframe, turn, and even invert a question that creates the depth and opening for authentic change. Questions take on an almost sacred dimension when they are valued for their own sake. This is in stark contrast to the common need for answers and quick formulaic action.

Choosing freedom and accountability. A second thread that courses through this book and has given coherence to all of Peter's work is the search for human freedom—freedom being the choice to be a creator of our own experience and accept the unbearable responsibility that goes with that. Out of this insight grows the idea that perhaps the real task of leadership is to confront people with their freedom. This may be the ultimate act of love that is called for from those who hold power over others.

Choosing our freedom is also the source of our willingness to choose to be accountable. The insight is that freedom is what creates accountability. Freedom is not an escape from accountability, as the popular culture so often misunderstands.

One more aspect of Peter's work that has informed my thinking about community is the idea that our willingness to care for the well-being of the whole arises when we are confronted with our freedom, and when we choose to accept and act on that freedom.

The Insights of Large Group Methodology: Designing for the Experience of Community

Over the last thirty years, a rather small group of people has become quite sophisticated in bringing large groups of people together (from fifty to five thousand at a time) to create visions, build strategy, define work processes, and set direction for institutions and communities. This body of knowledge has many names, but is generally called *large group methodology*. Although it is well established among expert practitioners, it has not found its way into the mainstream of how most leaders do planning and bring people together. These methods tend to be relegated to something that is pulled out on special occasions for special events. We treat these methods like sterling silver and use the stainless every day. This is a shame, for the difference between this kind of practice and the conventional way we bring people together is more like the difference between using sterling silver and eating with our hands.

These large group methods are too profound and too important to remain primarily in the hands of specialized experts. They need to be in the regular practice of community and institutional leaders. They are more than simply tools; they are the means of creating the experience of democracy and high engagement, which we say we believe in but rarely embody. As this thinking and practice grow, they have the potential to fundamentally change the nature of leadership, which would be a good thing.

Four of the innovators whose work is highlighted have been friends and teachers of mine for years. I reflect their thinking here only because I have been in many rooms with them. There are many others who have also changed the world and our thinking about bringing large groups of people together: Harrison Owen, Barbara Bunker, Billie Alban, Fred and Marilyn Emory, and Carolyn Lukensmeyer come to mind.

Future Search. Marvin Weisbord has created Future Search with Sandra Janoff. This structure begins with a scan of the environment and brings people into a conversation about the future they want to create. Marvin and Sandra have long understood the importance of the right question, the way to balance expert input with communal dialogue, and how to structure the flow of small group discussions into a collective outcome. They have also codified the distinction between solving problems and creating a future.

Conference Model. Dick and Emily Axelrod are design geniuses. They realized early on that if we can change the way we meet, we can change the way we live together. They know that learning best occurs when we structure meetings in a way that puts people in contact with each other so that they experience in a conference the same dilemmas they face in life. The

Axelrods create experiences that simulate the democratic, self-governing principles that, if taken seriously, can create large communities of committed and powerful people.

Whole-Scale Change. The late Kathie Dannemiller was another innovator in this movement. "One heart—one mind" was the spirit that she lived, and her goal was to bring that into an event where people assembled to create a new future. She had a faith in the collective capacity of employees and citizens that would put Thomas Jefferson to shame.

Her guiding question was "How will the world be different tomorrow as a result of our meeting today?" Like the others, she valued the question and held deep skepticism about answers. She also knew that the questions with the most power were the ones that touched the heart and spoke to what people were experiencing. If "What did you know and when did you know it?" defined the Watergate hearings, the question "What did you hear and how did you feel about that?" was at the core of her work.

Kathie wanted the whole system in the room, and then she constantly broke it into small groups. She advocated that the small group worked best when it was maximally diverse—meaning that each small group was a microcosm of the large system. This composition plus a broad-enough question results in people momentarily putting aside their own individual interests and beginning to care for the well-being of the whole.

The World Café. Finally, I want to talk about the work of Juanita Brown and her partner, David Isaacs. Their structure is called the World Café. Its gift is in its sophisticated simplicity. They begin by defining a large question that gets at the purpose of the gathering. Each small group focuses on the question, but in the Café method, the group sits at a round cocktail-sized table.

On each table is a flip-chart sheet or butcher paper and a marker for each person. As people talk, each writes on the paper in large letters the ideas worth retaining. At certain intervals, as in musical chairs (except that there are enough seats for all), one person stays as host at the table and the others go to different tables. The host summarizes for the new group what is on the paper, and the discussion continues. Eventually, the ideas from the tables are shared with the whole group. It is an elegant model to create convergence for a large group.

Now, my intent here is not to describe the full process for any of these innovative large group methods—I know that I do each a great injustice in my minimalist descriptions and acknowledgment. The intent is to define some of the essential elements that form the design basis of the large group work that informs our thinking about community transformation.

Each element of each large group method has profound implications for how people meet, how they create an alternative future, and how community can be developed in a sustainable way. What we may once have relegated as useful but incidental little "training exercises" now have a power beyond our imagination. They form a way of thinking and operating in community that, when matched with the philosophical insights of the others, give us the structure of belonging that we seek. Here is a brief summary of the power of their thinking:

> **Accountability and commitment.** The essential insight is that people will be accountable and committed to what they have a hand in creating. This insight extends to the belief that whatever the world demands of us, the people most involved have the collective wisdom to meet the requirements of that demand. And if we can get them together in the room, in the right context and with a few simple ground rules, the wisdom to create a future or solve a problem is almost always in the room. All you need to ensure this is to make sure the people in the room are a diverse and textured sample of the larger world you want to affect.
>
> This insight is an argument for collective intelligence and an argument against expensive studies and specialized expertise. That is why this thinking finds a skeptical ear from the academy, most expert consultants, and the leadership that espouses democracy but really only trusts patriarchy and cosmetic empowerment.
>
> **Learning from the stranger and one another.** The key to gathering citizens, leaders, and stakeholders is to create in the room a living example of how we want the future to be. This means we need as much diversity in the room as possible. The more strangers the better. One of the principles is that all voices need to be heard, but not necessarily all at one time or by everybody. What makes this succeed is that almost everything important happens in a small

group. This expresses another principle, that peer-to-peer interaction is where most learning takes place; it is the fertile earth out of which something new is produced. In this small group, you place the maximum mix of people's stories, values, and viewpoints, and in this way each group of six to twelve brings the whole system into that space.

Bias toward the future. The insights from large group methods have a bias toward the future and devote little or no time to negotiating the past or emphasizing those areas where we will never agree anyway. The most organizing conversation starter is "What do we want to create together?" So much for in-depth diagnoses, more studies, argument and negotiation, and waiting for the sponsorship or transformation of top leaders.

How we engage matters. The most important contribution of those who have developed these principles and insights is the idea that the way we bring people together matters more than our usual concerns about the content of what we present to people. How we structure the gathering is as worthy of attention as grasping the nature of a problem or focusing on the solutions we seek.

The gift to us from these masters of large group work is the belief that transformation hinges on changing the structure of how we engage each other. It is the insight that authentic transformation does not occur by focusing on changing individuals or being smart about political processes, which are based on advocacy of interests, hardball negotiation, or finding where the power resides and getting them on your side. The insights of these masters represent a dramatic shift from much of our conventional thinking, which, by the way, is not working that well.

The Bornstein-Cohen Insights: Scale, Speed, and Emergent Design

David Bornstein is a journalist who has written about the Grameen Bank in Bangladesh and other social innovations that have become large movements. Within the stories he tells in his books are some radical thoughts about how successful transformations came into being.

Small scale, slow growth. Not one of the examples David describes began as a government- or large-system-sponsored program. Each was begun with very little funding, no fanfare, and little concern about how to measure the outcomes. Each had a deeply committed and self-chosen leader with a commitment to make a difference in the lives of however many people they were able to reach.

Bornstein concluded that well-funded efforts, with clear outcomes, that spell out the steps to get there do not work. Changes that begin on a large scale, are initiated or imposed from the top, and are driven to produce quick wins inevitably produce few lasting results. This may be a clue to why our wars, such as those on drugs and poverty, have been consistently disappointing and sometimes have even produced more of what they sought to eliminate.

If you reflect on the stories of the successful leaders whom Bornstein documents, you realize that these entrepreneurs were committed enough and patient enough to give their projects time to evolve and find their own way of operating. There were years spent simply learning what structures, agreements, leadership, and types of people were required to be successful.

It was after the model had evolved and succeeded on its own terms that it began to grow, gain attention, and achieve a level of scale that touched large numbers of people.

This means that sustainable changes in community occur locally on a small scale, happen slowly, and are initiated at a grassroots level.

Emergent design. Allan Cohen is a brilliant strategy consultant who combines a deep understanding of the power of conversation with insights about the organic nature of design. A winning combination. Allan makes even more intentional and explicit the strategies that Bornstein has documented. Allan distinguishes between emergent strategies and destination or blueprint strategies. He says that effective change strategies obviously begin with a strong sense of purpose plus a commitment to bring something new into the world.

The key is what you do after that. Allan talks of two things: one is recognizing that organizations are always adapting and learning, even in the absence of big change initiatives. So a good place to start is by asking why the organization hasn't been moving naturally in a more desirable direction.

Then take modest steps to impact the conversations and relationships that are shaping the direction of change inherent in the organization. Watch what emerges, pause, reflect, and course-correct—then watch what emerges again. This is a crude definition of emergence.

The second insight from Allan is about changing the conditions under which an intention is acted on. He claims the ability to herd cats, which many have said is impossible. He does this by tilting the floor, which changes the conditions under which the cats are operating. Emergent strategies focus on conditions more than on behaviors or predictable goals. Ironically, the act of predicting the path may be the obstacle to achieving the purpose.

Allan's work on emergent design strongly emphasizes becoming clear on the purpose, the key to which is opening wide the possibility for a different future. He also gives importance to relatedness being the foundation of all achievement.

Combining the Insights

David Bornstein's stories are an expression of all the insights summarized here and woven throughout this book. For example, the efforts he talks about demonstrate the conditions leading to Alexander's quality of aliveness. They unfolded slowly and with great consciousness; then they became small whole centers in and of themselves, which finally, organically, began to combine with other centers to achieve some scale.

These efforts also had leaders who chose to live into Werner Erhard's concept of possibility. The ends seemed unachievable, and the commitment was not contingent on results. Each project created a new conversation about the people involved. Take Grameen Bank as an example. The founder declared that poor people were creditworthy and excellent entrepreneurs. This was simply a declaration of possibility and began a new conversation about poverty that shifted the context within which loans were made.

By this shift in context, Muhammad Yunus, founder of Grameen, embodied McKnight's observation that development is based on gifts, not deficiencies.

Grameen Bank also counted on the power of community and relatedness. Yunus and his bank created teams of borrowers (they called them *chapters*), in which each person's ability to receive a loan was dependent on the repayment by others in the group. A portion of each repayment went to fund the loans to other chapters and the well-being of the community. These small groups were the basic unit of borrowing, four women to a group. Not individuals, but the small group. Each small group also was required to operate as part of a larger community, so that the small groups could not become insular and act as if the boundary of their group was the edge of the earth. This is the essence of the large group methodologies.

There was for each team of borrowers a set of requirements that went beyond the money. They were accountable for producing a successful life for themselves and others, which is a correlate of Koestenbaum's understanding of freedom—that freedom and accountability are one and the same.

And all of this resulted in the wider benefits of having created social capital, as Putnam would term it. The participation of the women in the entrepreneurial venture affected all aspects of their lives and of their village. Eventually it would impact a nation.

Another example of these principles in action is the Family Independence Initiative (FII), which tracks the self-reported strengths, gifts, and initiatives of participating families and helps them see what they can create with a little help. FII provides matching funds and support for the progress that marginalized families produce on their own. They carefully avoid giving advice or thinking that they, the professionals, know what is best for a family. They are prescription-free. And it works.

So in this brief snapshot we have the core elements of the methods of collective transformation that follow. Integrating these insights gives us some basic conceptual elements for transforming communities. The reason to keep reading is to gain more form and depth to these ideas and apply them to our world, however large or small we may define it.

CHAPTER 2

Shifting the Context
for Community

The context that restores community is one of possibility, generosity, and gifts, rather than one of problem solving, fear, and retribution. A new context acknowledges that we have all the capacity, expertise, and resources that an alternative future requires. Communities are human systems given form by conversations that build relatedness. The conversations that build relatedness most often occur through associational life, where citizens show up by choice, and rarely in the context of system life, where citizens show up out of obligation. The small group is the unit of transformation and the container for the experience of belonging. Conversations that focus on stories about the past become a limitation to community; ones that are teaching parables and focus on the future restore community.

• • •

The move toward authentic community entails a shift in context. Context is an expression of the mental models we bring to our collective efforts. It is the set of beliefs—at times beliefs that we are unaware of—that dictate how we think, how we frame the world, what we pay attention to, and consequently how we behave. It is sometimes called a *worldview*. The existing dominant context is that we live in a world of scarcity, competition, and individualism.

Scarcity means that no matter how much we have, it is not enough. Whatever is needed, there is not enough to go around. Competition means that the world is, by its nature, rank ordered, top to bottom, a zero-sum game. Individualism means that you are on your own. Bootstrap time. It has us believe that people born on third base actually hit a triple. Individualism feeds the myth that there is such a thing as an autonomous human being.

This current context leads us to analyze deficiencies, define the gap between needs and aspiration, and believe that we need to produce more programs, more measurement, better planning, better problem solving, and stronger leadership.

The following are the shifts in context that would precede the movement into authentic community:

- We are a community of possibilities, not a community of problems.
- Community exists for the sake of belonging, and takes its identity from the gifts, generosity, and accountability of its citizens. It is not defined by its fears, its isolation, or its penchant for retribution.
- We currently have all the capacity, expertise, programs, leaders, regulations, and wealth required to end unnecessary suffering and create an alternative future.

Community is fundamentally an interdependent human experience given form by the conversation citizens hold among themselves. The history, buildings, economy, infrastructure, and culture are products of the conversations and social fabric of any community. The built and cultural environments are secondary gains of how we choose to be together.

Principles of Strategy

Shifting the context leads to certain principles of a strategy to build community:

- **The essential work is to build social fabric, both for its own sake and to enable chosen accountability among citizens.** When citizens care for each other, they become accountable to each other. Care and accountability create a productive community. The work is to design ways to bring citizens (including formal leaders, for they are citizens) together so that they experience the "quality of aliveness" Christopher Alexander writes about. This occurs by being highly attentive to the way that we gather.

- **Strong associational life is essential and central.** Associational life is how citizens choose to build connections for their own sake, sometimes for coffee, sometimes for a common purpose, like getting a stop sign put in. These sometime incidental encounters, or more regular meetings, are the core determinants for transformation. In associational life, creating connectedness becomes both an end and a means. Large established systems such as business, government, education, health care, and social services are important but are not essential to community transformation. For systems, building relatedness is mostly a means, not an end in itself.

- **Citizens using their power to convene other citizens create an alternative future.** A quality of aliveness occurs through change efforts that are energized by citizens and are organic or emergent in nature. A shift in the thinking and actions of citizens is more vital than a shift in the thinking and actions of institutions and formal leaders. This idea is in sharp contrast to the traditional beliefs that better leadership, more programs, new funding, new regulations, and more oversight are the path to a better future. All of these are necessary at times, but they do not have the power to create a fundamental shift.

- **The small group is the unit of transformation.** It is in the structure of how small groups gather that an alternative future will be created. This also means that we must set aside our concern for scale and our concern for speed. Scale, speed, and practicality are always the coded arguments for keeping the existing system in place. Belonging can occur through our membership in large groups, but this form of belonging reduces the power of citizens. Instead of surrendering our identity for the sake of belonging, we find in the small group a place that can value our uniqueness.

- **All transformation is linguistic, which means that we can think of community as essentially a conversation.** This means that if we want to change the community, all we have to do is change the conversation. The shift in conversation is from one of problems, fear, and retribution to one of possibility, generosity, and restoration. This is the new context that both creates strong social capital and is created by it.

The overarching intent of these principles is to create communities that operate out of a new context. Context clearly occurs as individual mind-sets, but it also exists as a form of collective worldview. Communities carry a context through the frequently repeated beliefs that citizens hold about the place where they live. The media is one carrier of this context, but does not create it.

If transformation is linguistic, then community building requires that we engage in a new conversation, one that we have not had before, one that can create an experience of aliveness and belonging. It is the act of engaging citizens in a conversation that allows us to act in concert and, equally important, to create accountability between citizens.

I am using the word *conversation* in a broad sense—namely, all the ways that we listen, speak, and communicate meaning to each other. So, in addition to speaking and listening, this meaning of *conversation* includes the architecture of our buildings and public spaces, the way we inhabit and arrange a room when we come together, and the space we give to the arts.

The Futility Context: Community as a Problem to Be Solved

To make a difference in our community, we must begin by naming the existing context and evolving to a way of thinking that leads to new conversations that produce a new context. It is the shift in conversation that increases social capital. Every time we gather has the potential to become a model of the future we want to create. If you really get this paragraph, you probably don't need to read any further.

Our current context is a long way from one of gifts, generosity, and accountability. The dominant context we now hold is one of deficiencies, interests, and entitlement. Out of this context grows the belief that the suffering of communities is a set of problems to be solved.

After we finish giving speeches about the virtues of our neighborhood and city, we love to elaborate their problems. We have studied and reported for years the problems of housing, health care, the environment, youth at risk, race, the disabled, poverty, unemployment, public education, the crisis in transportation, and drugs. These problems are studied by academics and fueled by talk radio and the AM band, which serve as places for hosts and citizens to argue, debate, and complain about who is right or wrong and who needs to change. And nowadays we have this thing called social media. Enough said.

Our love of problems runs deeper than just the joy of complaint, being right, or escape from responsibility. The core belief from which we operate is that an alternative or better future can be accomplished by more problem solving. We believe that defining, analyzing, and studying problems is the way to make a better world. It is the dominant mind-set of Western culture.

This context—that life is a set of problems to be solved—may actually limit any chance of the future being different from the past. The interest we have in problems is so intense that at some point we *take our identity from* those problems. Without them, it seems as though we would not know who we are as a community. Many of the strongest advocates for change would lose their sense of identity if the change they desired ever occurred.

Community-as-problems-to-be-solved has some benefits. It values the ability to implement, is big on doing, has a certain honesty about it, and worships tangible results as the ultimate blessing. You might say that this is what has gotten us this far. It is not that this (or any other) context is wrong; it just does not have the power to bring something new into the world.

To shift to some other context, we need to detach ourselves from the discussions of problems. One way to achieve this detachment is to see that what we now call problems are simply symptoms of something deeper.

For example, what we call "urban problems" are really symptoms of the breakdown of community. Barry Lopez, well-known author on the environment, lives in a town that several years ago suffered a terrible shooting at its high school. He wrote later that after all the TV cameras, advocates for and against gun control, grief counselors, and experts on youth and public education left town, the citizens could face the reality that the shooting was symptomatic of a breakdown in that community—a breakdown in citizens' capacity to create a place where this kind of tragedy could not happen. His analysis has stayed with me. The same could be said for the other tragic shootings in the United States, from Sandy Hook to Sutherland Springs, Las Vegas to Orlando, New York to San Bernardino.

The Limitations of Symptoms

The conventional approach to community building and development is to create programs, blueprints, and funding to keep us safe, keep us working, keep us housed and healthy. Every city has thousands of institutions, programs, and agencies all committed to serving the public good. Yet the needle for each of these in too many neighborhoods and cities refuses to move. Affordable housing, poverty, drug use, and obesity are moving in the wrong direction. From the standpoint of building community and social capital, these institutions and programs are treating the symptoms. Safety, jobs, housing, and the rest are symptoms of the unreconciled and fragmented nature of the community—what Lopez calls the breakdown of community. This fragmentation or breakdown creates a context in which trying to solve the symptoms only sustains them. Otherwise, why have we been working on these symptoms for so long and so hard? And even with so many successful programs, why have we seen too little fundamental change?

When we shift from talking about the problems of community to talking about the breakdown of community, something changes. *Naming the challenge as the "breakdown of community" opens the way for restoration.* Holding on to the view that community is a set of problems to be solved holds us in the grip of retribution.

At every level of society, we live in the landscape of retribution. The retributive community is sustained by several aspects of the modern community conversation, which I will expand on throughout the book: the marketing of fear and fault, gravitation toward more laws and oversight, an obsession with romanticized leadership, marginalizing hope and possibility, and devaluing associational life to the point of invisibility.

Getting Our Story About Story Straight

One form of the retributive community is the story we tell ourselves and each other about who we are. Getting clear about the nature of story is important in appreciating the power of the existing context, especially in those places where history and the past seem overridingly restraining.

Storytelling plays a noble and historic role in our lives and in society. Stories can give us a narrative to guide and instruct us. They are crucial to our knowing who we are; they provide a sense of identity. Some stories, however, become the limitation to creating anything new. Werner Erhard has been so insightful about this. We need to distinguish between the stories that give meaning to our lives and help us find our voice, and those that limit our possibility.

> In Russia, even the past is unpredictable.
>
> Author unknown

The stories that are useful and fulfilling are the ones that are metaphors, signposts, parables, and inspiration for the fullest expression of our humanity. They are communal teaching stories. Creation stories, wisdom stories, sometimes personal stories that have a mythic quality, even if they come from the person sitting next to you.

Theater, movies, song, literature, and art are storytelling of the highest order. These are the mediums for building an individual sense of what it means to be human. The arts are an essential part of the story of what it means to be a human being and a community.

There are other kinds of stories that in their telling become a limitation. Limiting stories are personal versions of the past. They are stories about the conclusions we drew from events that happened to us. Other limiting stories are those that are rehearsed or make the point that the future will be a slightly modified continuation of the past out of which the story arose. Stories of this nature place us as victims of events or even fate.

Limiting stories are the ones that present themselves as if they were true. Facts. Our stories of our own past are heartfelt and yet are fiction. All we know that is true is that we were born. We may know for sure who our parents, siblings, and other key players in our drama were. But our version of all of them, the meaning and memory that we narrate to all who will listen, is our creation. Made up. Fiction. And this is good news, for it means that a new story can be concocted any time we choose.

Same with community. The stories of violence, crime, and wrongdoing that are constantly told are also fiction. The events may have happened, but the versions that let those events define who we are as a community—such as whether it is safe to go downtown, whether we need new leaders, whether people in this place are friendly, whether we are headed up or down—are all fiction. The decision to tell those stories over and over again as if they were defining truths creates the limitation against an alternative future.

This is why therapy and healing are really processes of re-remembering the past in a more forgiving way. The willingness to own up to the fictional nature of our story is where the healing begins. And where the possibility of restoration resides.

In this way, restoration can be considered the willingness to complete and extract the power out of the current story we have of our community and our place in it. This creates an opening to produce a new collective story. A new story based on restorative community. One of possibility, generosity, accountability.

CHAPTER 3

The Stuck Community

The existing community context is one that markets fear, assigns fault, and worships self-interest. This context supports the belief that the future will be improved with new laws, more oversight, and stronger leadership. Possibility thinking and associational life are marginalized, relegated to human interest and side stories in the media. The corporate model is the modern ideal, and the economy is the center story. The story in the stuck community defines the role of the media as framer of the debate. In community building, we need to realize that what the media reports is a reflection, not the cause, of the conversation that citizens currently hold.

• • •

To create a new story, we first need to come to terms with the current one. This begins by naming it. The story of the stuck community can be heard both in the dominant public debate and also in what we talk about to each other each day. It is important to understand that there is a hidden agenda in every story. This agenda is a point to be made, a political belief about what is important, that stays constant regardless of the events of the day.

Marketing Fear and Fault

The overriding characteristic of the stuck community is the decision to broadcast all the reasons we have to be afraid. This is a kind of advertising that exploits the fear we have of violence, of the urban core, of terrorism, of African Americans and other ethnic groups, of immigrants, of those who are poor or undereducated, of other religions, and of other countries. It seems as though the lead story of every local evening newscast is about crime and human suffering, and if our city had none that day, then we hear how somewhere else in the world someone was murdered, bombed, killed in an accident, or abducted from what was once thought to be a safe place. What we are hearing is the marketing of fear.

In the telling, we are willing to sacrifice the wholeness and dignity of a person for the sake of capturing the emotion or drama of the moment. The marketing of fear thrusts a microphone in the face of someone who has just suffered an irreplaceable loss and asks, "How do you feel?" It is the commercialization of suffering for the sake of profit. Not that complicated.

> When I was deputy press secretary at the White House, our credibility was so bad we couldn't believe our own leaks.
>
> Bill Moyers

The marketing of fear is not just for profit; it also holds a political agenda. Fear justifies the retributive agenda, fundamentalist in the extreme, that has been on the rise for some time. The retributive agenda believes that a just and civil society is one that gives priority to restraints, consequences, and control, and underlines the importance of rules. It gets packaged as spiritual values, family values, the American Way, love it or leave it, all under the umbrella of law and order. It helps build the incarceration industry and the protection industry, it creates a platform that enables those in power to expand their belief system, and it discounts the rehabilitation industry. Fear forms the basis of our recent foreign policy and drives much of our legislation. Fear also fuels the allure of suburban life and is a subtle but clear argument against diversity and inclusion.

• • •

In addition to marketing fear, the stuck community markets fault. When there is a human tragedy, most of the energy goes into finding who was to blame. There is a retributive search for responsibility and a corresponding defense from the players claiming their innocence. This blame marketing rests on the belief that if we can assign blame and find cause, it is useful to society and somehow reassures us that the tragedy won't happen again. To me, this is irrational thinking. What is missing here is a recognition of the complexity of human affairs, an acknowledgment of the paradoxical and accidental nature of life. There is no insurance policy against the human condition.

Out of the decision to dwell on fear and fault, the community is stuck in a context that holds the following:

- We are a community of problems to be solved. Those who can best articulate the problems and who can best articulate the solutions dominate the conversation.

- The future is defined by the interplay of self-interests, dependent on the accountability of leaders, and controlled by a small number of wealthy and powerful people, commonly lumped into the category we call "they."

- Community action is aimed at eliminating the sources of our fear. We aim at a set of needs and deficiencies. In order to eliminate our fear and respond to the neediness of our people, we try harder at what we have been doing all along. We lock down neighborhoods, build more prisons, and reduce tolerance to zero. We call for better measurements, more expertise, more funding, better leadership, stronger consequences, and more protection. We are committed to trying harder at what is not working.

Ramping Up Laws and Oversight

When something goes wrong, we carry the illusion that after we find the guilty party, some kind of legislation or change in policy will prevent the crime or accident from happening again. We are stuck in the belief that we can legislate the future and mandate morality. In Cincinnati, we passed an ordinance that street people had to be licensed to ask passersby for money. The idea was that somehow I now would be comfortable going downtown knowing that the person asking for money had been certified and approved by the city council. Now even panhandling was professionalized. The ordinance did not bring more people into town at night.

A corollary to passing more laws is the push for more oversight. We think that more watching improves performance. All the evidence is to the contrary, for most high-performing communities and organizations are heavily self-regulating. My favorite quote on this is "Research causes cancer in rats." It is reasonable to understand that the act of oversight may in fact increase the very thing that is being watched with the intent of reducing it.

The political agenda of the stuck community says that citizens and employees are incapable of monitoring themselves and controlling each other, and that more careful oversight, institutionally mandated and installed, will build community and provide for the common good. It is in fact an argument against building community. It ends up leaving us more dependent on security specialists and professionalized control. It provides the business case for monarchy. Someone to watch over me.

Romanticizing Leadership

Carole Schurch was taking care of the logistics of a conference on transformation. She opened the event by announcing, "The restrooms are down the hall on the left, lunch will be at 1:00 p.m., dinner is at 8:00 p.m., and the conference will be over tomorrow afternoon. Let me know if I can help you with anything and also let me know what time your mother is picking you up!"

We love our habit of dependency and accept the culture of retribution because it reinforces the case for strong leaders—"strong" being the code word for autocratic, a message our culture is increasingly willing to accede to. We are fascinated with our leaders. We speak endlessly, both in the public conversation and privately, about the rise and fall of leaders. The agenda this sustains is that leaders are cause and all others are effect. That all that counts is what leaders do. That leaders are the leverage point for building a better community. That they are foreground, while citizens, followers, players, and anyone else not in a leadership position are background. This is a deeply patriarchal agenda, and it is this love of leaders that limits our capacity to create an alternative future. It proposes that the only real accountability in the world is at the top. They are the only ones worth talking about.

The effect of buying in to this view of leadership is that it lets citizens off the hook and breeds citizen dependency and entitlement. It undermines the development of a culture where each is accountable for their community. The attention on the leader makes good copy; it gives us someone to blame and thereby declares our innocence. In its own way, it reinforces individualism, putting us in the stance of waiting for the cream to rise, wishing for a great individual to bring light where there is darkness. It is possible to admire and be inspired by great leaders, even bosses, but we need to resist the projection that they can produce a change in the conditions that concern us. Each of us is accountable for our small piece of creating better conditions. When we project that on a leader, power gets abused and disappointment is inevitable.

What is missing or dismissed here are the community-building insights about how groups work, the power of relatedness, what occurs when ordinary people get together. We write communal possibility off as just another meeting, the blind leading the blind, citizens coming together to pool ignorance or to speak "truth to power," which is just a complaint session in evening clothes.

As an aside, some reasons for discounting the power of citizens are well founded, for most of the time when citizens come together it makes no difference. That's because they operate under the retributive principles that I am trying to describe in this section. They want to define the problem, find fault, elaborate fear, demand control-oriented action, and point to leaders. Many citizens get engaged in community only when they are angry.

If we keep engaging citizens in this traditional way, then no amount of involvement will make a difference. The way we currently gather has no transformational power. This is what needs to change, for if we do not change the way citizens come together, if we do not shift the context under which we gather and do not change the methodology of our gatherings, then we will have to keep waiting for great leaders, and we will never step up to the power and accountability that is within our grasp.

Marginalizing Possibility

Given the dominant context that values scarcity, leadership, individualism, fear, and fault, anything positive or hopeful becomes an anomaly. An exception, an accident. To choose possibility means that we have to confront cynicism. Journalism, human services, corrections, and public safety are professions which claim that their cynicism comes from constant contact and familiarity with the dark side of society. This ignores the reality that what you see comes from what you choose to look at. Decide that all the news fit to print is about problems, and that is what you get. In the retributive culture, cynicism is the norm and becomes the lead story. Cynicism justifies retribution. Retribution is fueled by cynicism.

In this context, possibility and vision become buried in the middle section of the news, or become an upbeat pat on the back as the anchor goes off the air. Possibility and faith are seen as threatening because they are an indictment of cynicism. So when citizens do find a way to use their gifts, or commit to something thought impossible, or bring faith and gratitude into the world, it is not by accident that the story is reduced to a "human interest" piece—the kiss of death when it comes to changing our context. Many reporters do not even consider these stories journalism.

When labeled "human interest," possibility doesn't qualify as news. It is a feel-good diversion. Something to calm our nerves. Possibility and the faith that supports it may be strong declarations for the individual, but for the collective, they are neutered and treated as merely charming. Mainstream journalism treats us as passive spectators and is a profession which thinks that its role is to speak truth to power. It worships the sensational and the tragic. What bleeds is what leads. This is costing the profession its audience. Especially since every individual is now a publisher. We need to support the efforts of a journalism committed to what is working. Think of the Solutions Journalism Network, the citizen journalism movement, NewScoop in Calgary, *Kolbe Times*. Small signs of a shift in thinking.

Possibility also gets undermined by being confused with optimism. Even when leaders speak to the possibility of our community, in the stuck community we consider it a motivational speech, a sales pitch, a bootstrap keynote to make us feel better and lift our spirits from what we call reality.

But possibility is not a prediction or a goal; it is a choice to bring a certain quality into our lives. Optimism, which *is* a prediction about the future, has no power. Pessimism is equally irrelevant.

The ways in which possibility is marginalized underline the importance of context. All that does not confirm the prevailing mind-set is made marginal and cute. This is why, if you want to create an alternative future, you have to shift the context, for all that disconfirms the current context will be discarded. We need to shift what is considered "reality." For example, what if we see the media as a reflection of who we are, and choose to listen primarily to media that promote learning and possibility, document miracles, and report on a different agenda, and call it the "new reality"? Les Ihara, a longtime state senator in Hawaii, says that what is needed is "a shift in the ground of being that reports the news."

Devaluing Associational Life

John McKnight has studied communities for thirty years and found that community is built most powerfully by what he calls "associational life," referring to the myriad ways citizens come together to do good work and serve the public interest. Whether in clubs, associations, informal gatherings, special events, or just on the street or at breakfast, neighborly contact constitutes an uncounted and unnoticed glue and connection that makes good communities work.

The stuck community essentially discounts associational life and instead values, and even glorifies, the "system" life, especially the private sector and corporate mind-set. This context is so pervasive that we have become anaesthetized to it. Although there is a growing awareness of the cost of this mind-set (see David Korten's work, listed at the end of the book), we still act as if what is good for business is good for the country.

Here are some ways in which we discount associational life, the place where the social fabric is built:

- **The only true measure of community is its economic prosperity according to traditional measures.** We seek the American dream, streets paved with gold. The only good news that makes the news is when Toyota decides to build a plant in our town. Communities will justify spending infinite amounts of money to keep sports teams because they are theoretically good for the economy. Job creation is the final argument for most of our mistakes, especially when we destroy the neighborhood economy. We measure the neighborhood and the person by their average annual income.

- **We name social services and institutions that serve the public good "not for profits."** "Not for profit" means that service and generosity are defined by what they are not. What kind of identity and esteem does this establish for the choice for service and care for community? Can you imagine introducing yourself as the name you are *not?* "Hello, my name is not Alice." "Well, I would like you to meet my friend, not Roger." There is no identity in that. Nothing memorable or recognizable next time we meet. There is a movement to call it the "public benefit" sector. Not such a bad thing.

- **Associations are under constant pressure to be more corporate: to merge, become more efficient, submit to external oversight, measure harder, and submit to greater accountability.** These are core values in the private sector. A natural outgrowth of this is the way many foundations, which exist for the sake of community service, treat corporations as their clients. In the philanthropic world, you also hear people talk about their "return on social investment." We use the language of commerce when talking about the field of generosity.

- **The public benefit sector makes front-page news only when there is scandal.** The head of a large agency who spends funds on limousines and high living is on the front page for days. When the same agency softens the landing for people in a tragedy or turns people's lives around, the story is at best a footnote.

- **We marginalize compassion in the public conversation.** Here's an example: As an effort to build the image and well-being of the city, Go Cincinnati is about streetcars, housing development, and attracting new businesses. It sells hard the strengths of the city, including the arts, entertainment, and sports attractions. All good things to sell and essential to a city that works. What is missing in this conversation and sales pitch is the compassion of a city. Having a large number of social services in a neighborhood is seen as a weakness, not a selling point. The view is that if people need help, if they are vulnerable or in crisis, it is a communal liability. The generosity that serves these people goes unmentioned as an asset.

Reinforcing Self-Interest and Isolation

These dimensions of the way we talk about our community and the stories we repeatedly tell about our community work together to create an insular mentality. Under the siege of fear, fault, and the rest, people and institutions build a wall around themselves and are primarily concerned with their own interests and survival. This gives us a community in which each sector—business, education, government, social service, health care—is so focused on its own affairs that those who choose to commit to the well-being of the whole have a difficult time gaining a foothold.

And what exists for our institutions is reinforced by citizens. Citizens mostly get engaged when something threatens their backyard. They show up in public settings when they are angry; they become activated only by local, next-door interests.

To summarize, the context of retribution and the story that grows out of it cause our attempts to build community to be what actually keeps it unchanged. Our retributive approach to the symptoms of poverty, violence, homelessness, and cynicism does not create these symptoms, but does interfere with their changing. Retribution by its nature serves to fragment community and reduce social capital. The side effect is that each citizen's accountability for the well-being of community is reduced. When the context is retributive, reduced accountability and diminished social capital are the direct outgrowths of our very efforts to improve community. And this mostly occurs as an unintended consequence, for no one holds a fragmented community as a goal.

The Media

As a key messenger of context in the stuck community, the media takes its cue from citizens and makes its living from the call for retribution. The public conversation most visible to us is the interaction between what we citizens want to hear and the narrative put forth by the media. But it is too easy to blame the media for valuing entertainment over news and for selling fear and problems over generosity and possibility. It is more useful to see that the media is a reflection of who we, as citizens, have become.

The news is most usefully understood as the daily decisions about what is newsworthy. This is a power that goes way beyond simply informing us. The agenda in each story defines what is important, and in doing this, it promotes an identity for a community.

> The problem, of course, was that Baba saw the world in black and white. And he got to decide what was black and white.
>
> Khaled Hosseini,
> *The Kite Runner*

This means that the real importance of the media is not in the typical debate over the quality, balance, or even accuracy of what is reported. These vary with the channel, the network, the newspaper, the website. They vary depending on having the resources to get the whole story, the market segment the source is aiming at, and its editorial agenda. What is most important, and the power that is most defining, is the power of the media to decide what is worth talking about. As British newspaper pioneer Lord Northcliffe once said, "News is what somebody somewhere wants to suppress; all the rest is advertising."

The media's power is the power to name the public debate. Or, in other words, the power to name "reality." This is true for the mainstream as well as online media.

Plus there are new players in the media landscape. The Internet, the social networks, the blogosphere have invaded the world we once called news. While the traditional media still define what the story is about, the texture and color come from every direction, and the most powerful players on social media sites such as Twitter, Instagram, and Facebook take retribution, blame, and accusation to the extreme. Technology is often held up as the answer to the future, but at this point it mostly just amplifies the dominant story.

The point is this: citizens have the capacity to change the community story, to reclaim the power to name what is worth talking about, to bring a new context into being. Those of us who create the current dominant context for the community conversation drive the conditions that nurture a retributive context and a retributive community. If we do not choose to change this context and the strategies that follow from it, we will produce no new outcomes for our institutions, neighborhoods, and towns.

CHAPTER 4

The Restorative Community

Restoration comes from the choice to value possibility and relatedness over problems, needs, self-interest, and the rest of the stuck community's agenda. It hinges on the accountability chosen by citizens and their willingness to connect with each other around promises they make to each other.

Restoration is created by the kinds of conversations we initiate with each other. These conversations are the leverage point for an alternative future. The core question that underlies each conversation is "What can we create together?" Shifting the context from retribution to restoration will occur through the use of language that moves in the following directions: from problems to possibility; from fear and fault to gifts, generosity, and abundance; from law and oversight to social capital and chosen accountability; from the dominance of corporation and systems to the centrality of associational life; and from leaders to citizens.

• • •

In contrast to the isolating effects of retribution, a restorative experience, relationship, or community produces new energy rather than holding us in place. Restoration is associated with the quality of aliveness and wholeness that Christopher Alexander talks about. This quality is not only in the artifacts, buildings, and spaces that he refers to but also in the gatherings and conversations we choose to create. The energy crisis we face is not so much about fossil fuels as it is about the calcified experience that is too often created by the way we hold conversations, both publicly and when we come together in more private settings.

Restorative community is activated by language of connection and relatedness and belonging, spoken without embarrassment. It recognizes that taking responsibility for one's own part in creating the present situation is the critical act of courage and engagement, which is the axis around which the future rotates. The essence of restorative community building is not economic prosperity or the political discourse or the capacity of leadership; it is citizens' willingness to own up to their contribution or agency in the current conditions, to be humble, to choose accountability, and to have faith in their own capacity to make authentic promises to create the alternative future.

This all matters because to achieve what we seek hinges on the question of accountability. Asking who will be accountable is about asking who will stand up to be counted. In whose hands does transformation rest? It is not by chance that in the United States we have more people in jails and prisons than any other country in the world. We are dominated by the punitive mind-set of consequences, of setting examples, of assigning blame when suffering occurs. These are the practices of an imperial culture, which is nourished by fear. Retributive cultures claim to increase accountability, but they actually can't deliver it. Accountability is always a choice, what someone does when no one else is looking. Handcuffs do not get the job done.

This means that the essential aspect of the restoration of community is a context in which each citizen chooses to be accountable rather than entitled. This inverts the common use of the word *accountability*. It is most often used as a burden, a basis for future liability. Not necessarily so.

Accountability is the willingness to care for the whole, and it flows out of the kind of conversations we have about the new story from which we want to take our identity. It means we have conversations about what we can do to create the future. Entitlement is a conversation about what others can or need to do to create the future for us.

Restoration begins when we think of community as a possibility, a declaration of the future that we choose to live into. This idea of a communal possibility is distinct from what we commonly call an individual possibility. Community is something more than a collection of individual longings, desires, or possibilities. The communal possibility has its own landscape and its own dynamics, requirements, and points of leverage. In the individualistic world we live in, we can congregate a large collection of self-actualized people and still not hold the idea or experience of community.

The communal possibility rotates on the question "What can we create together?" This emerges from the social space we create when we are together. It is shaped by the nature of the culture within which we operate but is not controlled by it. This question of what we can create together is at the intersection of possibility and accountability. Possibility without accountability results in wishful thinking. Accountability without possibility creates more of what we have now, which ultimately turns to despair, for even if we know we are creating the world we exist in, we cannot imagine its being any different from the past that got us here.

Example: The Clermont Counseling Center

Tricia Burke was the director of the Clermont Counseling Center. She completely understood the destructive power of labeling and categorizing human beings. Rare for one in a leadership position in a labeling industry. One of her programs was for women in abusive relationships who are survivors of domestic violence. She called this program Women of Worth. What's in a name . . . everything.

The counseling center also ran a mental health facility. The center exemplified most of the elements of freedom, choice, transforming language, and small group belonging discussed in this book. In the mental health program were clients labeled as paranoid schizophrenic, bipolar, and delusional, and people who had a history of state hospital stays. For the center to bill Medicaid for their services, the services must be "medically necessary." This means that the center was required to certify each client's illness and medicalize all of the center's services in order to be reimbursed.

In the eyes of Tricia and her staff, many of the most effective healing efforts come from actions that are not really medical interventions. What are often most healing are the ways that people in programs discover how to have fun in what they do and feel embraced and surrounded by the support of others like themselves. The sense of belonging that accrues is as healing as traditional treatment. This sort of thing is not a legitimate program activity in the eyes of Medicaid. To keep Medicaid funding, the center was required to name and place a disease on the head of each person.

Despite this, Tricia and her staff decided to change the conversation at Clermont in dramatic ways. They gave up the Medicaid funding for their "partial hospital day treatment" program and put the clients in charge of the day program. Staff were reassigned to other programs. In doing this, Tricia changed the message to clients from one focusing on their liabilities to one focusing on their possibilities. The organizing questions to members—no longer patients—were "What do you like to do?" and "How do you want to fill your day?" The traditional hospital experiences were maintained, but these questions were the organizing principles that guided the healing process.

The strategy then was to treat members as if they had the capacity to design and structure a good portion of their own time. Phoenix Place, the new name the members chose for this effort, became a member-controlled self-governing program. There was only one paid staff member—Kim Hensley, the director of the program—and many of the governance and program decisions were placed in the hands of members.

In the first year, the members came up with ingenious answers to the question "What can we create together?" For example:

- They formed and chose an executive committee for themselves.
- They organized a wellness activity.
- They volunteered their services to an animal shelter.
- They wanted to travel, so they decided to open a snack shop to earn money.
- When Phoenix Place received a grant to offer medication education for other mentally ill folk in five counties, the members provided it themselves.
- When Ohio state legislators were invited to visit the facility, the members wanted time with them to make the point that people who have mental illness are not their illness; they are much more than their illness.
- They were no longer afraid to talk about their lives; they came out of the closet.
- The group started training police on the nature of mental illness— what it is like to hear voices, for example. They taught the police how to approach people having an incident and what language to use.

- They started a journaling process, which they called WildSpirits, to give voice to what it feels like to be in the dark hole of despair and find your way out, and to express their healing by writing about hope, gratitude, and love.

At the end of the first year of Phoenix Place, its members felt pride in what they had created; they had jobs to do and had regained some of the roles they had lost in the larger society. Most of all, they had begun once again to have hopes and dreams about their future.

Eventually they outgrew the small house for Phoenix Place, so they set about raising money for a bigger one by working the concession stands at the Reds and Bengals games—and years later their dream came true. When it did, they wrote a grant proposal to make a video to tell their story.

Of course, the story of Phoenix Place, and others like it, is not all about success and victory. Along the way, Tricia says, it took patience and encouragement to help Phoenix members shift their thinking to believing that they could run their own program. In the beginning, they were angry and felt they were being abandoned. They even picketed the center. Helping them break free of their dependency was difficult.

Here is a part I especially like: As part of a program on positive psychology, one exercise was for individuals to complete a questionnaire about their strengths. The members noted that this was the first time in their lives they had ever taken a test and gotten good news from the results.

The transition from patient to citizen is always difficult—for all of us, not just labeled people. And the trajectory is not always smooth. For example, the departure of the original director of Phoenix Place caused anxiety and worry. The member-led executive committee began to act superior, controlling, and judgmental, and some of the spirit of community waned. In other words, the committee started to function like most traditional executive committees. Eventually, this center and its radical values were absorbed into a more traditional institution of service. Which underscores the power of the dominant context.

Nothing in Phoenix Place's ending detracts from what it created or what it meant to the people it touched. What is important for each of us is what conclusions we draw from the example, which is the point of context: whatever we conclude is ours to manufacture.

Lessons from Restorative Justice

Phoenix Place gives us a powerful model of what a restorative community can look like. When I say "restorative," I am not talking about returning to a prior time, fixing up an old building, or seeking to recapture a culture that we think once existed. Restoration is about healing our woundedness—in community terms, healing our fragmentation and incivility. It is only out of this healing that something new can emerge.

I have been attracted for some time by the way *restorative* is used in the criminal justice system, which I learned from Barry Stuart, Lee Rush, and others who have created the restorative justice movement. They have given a powerful structure to restoration, and they have done it in a most unlikely place. The intent of restoration in the criminal justice system is to provide a more reconciled path for both the offender and the victim of a crime. This becomes an option for the victim to choose and for the offender to agree to. It also gives a voice to the community, for the community is also wounded by a crime.

There are several steps to restoration. They all occur in a meeting. The offender admits to the crime, the offender and the victim and their families talk of the cost and damage the crime has caused to all their lives, the offender apologizes for the offense, the offender promises not to do it again, and the offender agrees to some form of restitution for the damage caused.

Finally, the victim and their family decide whether to forgive the offender and accept the restitution. If they decide to forgive, then the representatives of the community have a voice in deciding whether to allow the offender to go free and rejoin the community. If the victim and family decide not to forgive, then the offender goes through the regular criminal justice process. On a global scale, restorative justice is similar to the practices of the Truth and Reconciliation Commission in South Africa.

These steps contain many of the elements of community building. It is not so much the methodology that concerns us here, but rather the context and spirit that these movements offer us. They show that an alternative to retribution is possible and has worked in the world. This spirit of restoration promises a different future for our communities.

Community as Conversation

The idea of community restoration becomes concrete when we grasp the importance of language. When we do, we can see how our language, or conversation, is the action step that makes creating an alternative future possible. Stated simply, we can begin to think of our communities as nothing more or less than a conversation. If we can accept the idea that all real change is a shift in narrative—a new story as opposed to the received dominant story—then the function of citizenship, or leadership, is to invite a new narrative into existence. Narrative begins with a ride on the wave of conversation. For greatest effect, we need a new conversation with people we are not used to talking to.

Every community has its buildings, leaders, schools, and landscape, but for the moment let us say that these are not what make a community unique or define its identity. Instead we decide to declare that the aspect of a community that gives it a new possibility is simply the conversation that citizens choose to have with themselves. Jane Jacobs, world expert on neighborhoods, understands this. When she was asked why she thought Portland, Oregon, has been so successful in creating a habitable community, she said that the only thing unique about Portland is that "Portlanders love Portland." In our terms here, it was the conversation Portlanders had with each other about their town that made the difference.

Thus if we speak of change or transformation in our city or town—in my case, Cincinnati—we are referring to the conversation that is occurring in that town. We highlight the conversation community members have with themselves not because it is the whole picture, but because it is the part of the picture that is most amenable to change.

This means that the alternative future we speak of takes form when we realize that the only powerful place from which to take our identity may be the story we hold about ourselves and our collective way of being together. We begin the process of restoration when we understand that our well-being is defined simply by the nature and structure and power of our conversation.

The future of a community then depends on a choice between a retributive conversation (a problem to be solved) and a restorative conversation (a possibility to be lived into). Restoration is a possibility brought into being by choosing that kind of conversation. And with that conversation, restoration becomes real and tangible, for once we have declared a possibility, and done so with a sense of belonging and in the presence of others, that possibility has been brought into the room and thus into the institution, into the community.

The key phrase here is "in the presence of others." When declared publicly, heard and witnessed by others with whom we have a common interest, at a moment when something is at stake, a possibility is a critical element of communal transformation. This public conversation creates a larger relatedness and transcends a simply individual transformation. In the faith world, this is similar to what has been called bearing witness. We are bringing that into secular practice. Conversations of possibility gone public are not all that restores, but without them, personal and private conversations of possibility have no political currency and therefore no communal power.

The Shift

To summarize the story line to this point, our conversations and gatherings have the power to shift the context from retributive community to restorative community. This occurs through questions and dialogue that move us in the following directions:

- From conversations about problems to ones of possibility

- From conversations about fear and fault to ones of gifts, generosity, and abundance

- From a bet on law and oversight to a preference for building the social fabric and chosen accountability

- From seeing the corporation and systems as central to change to seeing associational life as central

- From a focus on leaders to a focus on citizens

What these have in common is the movement from centrism and individualism to collectivism and interdependent communalism. This shift has important consequences for our communities. It offers to return politics to public service and restore our trust in leadership. It moves us from having faith in professionals and those in positions of authority to having faith in our neighbors. It takes us into a context of hospitality, wherein we welcome strangers rather than believing we need to protect ourselves from them. It changes our mind-set from valuing what is efficient to valuing belonging. It helps us leave behind our penchant for seeing our disconnectedness as an inevitable consequence of modern life and moves us toward accountability and citizenship.

CHAPTER 5

Taking Back Our Projections

Citizens become powerful when they choose the context within which they operate. This choosing is difficult because we are seeking an alternative to the received wisdom of the culture. Choosing our own language of context, rather than aligning with the language of the dominant culture, puts the choice into our own hands. It acknowledges that our mind-set, even our worldview, is subjective and therefore amenable to change. There is a cost to this—namely, we are subject to doubt and at times loneliness. It is the path of a pioneer.

To choose a context conducive to citizenship, we first need to understand the idea of communal projection. Projection is the act of attributing qualities to others that we deny within ourselves. It is expressed in the way we label others and then build diagnostic categories and whole professions around the labeling. The shift away from projection and labeling provides the basis for defining what we mean by authentic citizenship—which is to hold ourselves accountable for the well-being of the larger community and to choose to own and exercise collective power rather than defer or delegate it to others.

• • •

Here is a way of thinking about the shift in context from retribution to restoration. We begin with going deeper into what it means to choose to be accountable, not just for ourselves but for the world. The reason the retributive context cannot improve the conditions it tries to heal is that it talks a lot about accountability but does not embody it. The context of retribution itself is actually an ongoing argument against accountability.

This happens each time I want to see a change in "those people." Those people can be supervisors, top management, the mayor, immigrants, people living in poverty—the list is endless. When I develop prescriptions for "their" transformation, I am making them the cause of our troubles. I am expressing the belief that if "those people" were different, our organization, our community would be better.

This is the attraction of the marketing of fear and fault and our love of leadership. It is a way of seeking control through the belief that something or someone else is the problem and that the someone else needs to do something different before anything can profoundly get better. And the clincher is that, as holders of the dominant narrative, we believe we know what that something different is. This is the colonial nature of most of our public conversations. On a large scale, it is what drives Great Britain out of the European Union. It is what wants to build a wall to keep the stranger out. It is why my mother was angry with her brother for forty years.

To inquire more deeply into this shift in context, we need to focus on the distinction between culture and context. The common thinking holds that transformation requires a culture change. I am talking here about context, not culture. The reason I use the word *context* rather than *culture* is to construct our stance as a matter of choice. Culture is a set of shared values that emerges from the history of experience and the story that is produced out of that. It is the past that gives us our identity and corrals our behavior in order to preserve that identity. Context is the way we see the world. See the world, not remember the world.

We conventionally think that our view of the world is based on history, events, and evidence, and this pattern is treated as fact and is decisive. It is called fact but is only a collective memory, which in the glare of the midday sun I would irreverently call fiction. If this thing we call context were fact, then it would not be amenable to transformation.

If context were inevitable and purely based on fact, then we would be condemned to live in fear. We are constantly being sold the fear curriculum so that, in time, we begin to think the context of fear is for good cause and data based. In reality, fear rises and falls for more reasons than events would dictate. If we can entertain the thought that fear is the curriculum of the patriarchal element of our culture, then we can understand that the dominant fear conversation is as much a result of marketing and product promotion as it is a response to facts. In the domain of public safety, for instance, there is little relationship between the crime rate and people's attitude about danger. There is evidence that many kinds of crime went down in many major cities in the late 1990s and have stayed down to this present moment. But while crime went down, the public's fear of crime went up. Why? Because while crime was going down, the reporting of crime went up. So the determinant of our fear is partly the retributive agenda, which leads to reporting about how dangerous the world is and, more important, our choice to buy the story.

Here is the point: in the retributive context, we act as though fear, fault, dependency on leaders, cynicism, and indifference to associational life are evidence based. If we are committed to a future distinct from the past, then we treat them as a matter of choice, and we call this way of thinking context, not culture.

Projection and Labeling

If the fear-retribution cycle is a matter of choice and not an inevitable result of culture, then we have to face the fact that the choice to inhale it must mean it offers us payoffs.

One payoff for believing that problems and the suffering in our cities are the inevitable products of modern life and culture is that it lets us off the hook. The payoff begins the moment we believe that problems reside in others and that these others are the ones who need to change. We displace or assign to others certain qualities that in fact have more to do with us than with them. This is called *projection,* an idea most of us are quite familiar with. I discuss it here because if we do not take back our projection, a new context and conversation are simply not possible. The essence of our projection is that it places accountability for an alternative future on others. This is the payoff of stereotyping, prejudice, and a bunch of "isms" that we are all familiar with. This is what produces the "other." The reward is that it takes the pressure off of us. It is a welcome escape from our freedom. We project onto leaders the qualities or disappointments that we find too much to carry ourselves. We project onto the stranger, the wounded, the enemy those aspects of ourselves that are too much to own.

Projection denies the fact that my view of the "other" is my creation, and this is especially true with how we view our communities and the people in them. Most simply, how I view the other is an extension or template of how I view myself. This insight is the essence of being accountable. To be accountable is to act as an owner and creator of what exists in the world, including the light and dark corners of my own existence. It is the willingness to focus on what we can do in the face of whatever the world presents to us. Accountability does not project or deny; accountability is the willingness to see the whole picture that resides within, even what is not so pretty.

> "You pushed my buttons."
> "I know, but I didn't install them."
> Author unknown

We are generally familiar with these ideas from the psychology of projection for individuals, and the point here is that projection also works more broadly at the level of profession, institution, and community.

Take poverty, for example. When we see low-income people, we focus on their needs and deficiencies, and that is all we see. We think their poverty is central to who they are, and that is all they are. We believe that the poor have created that condition for themselves. We view them with charity or pity and wring our hands at their plight. At this moment we are projecting our own vulnerability onto the poor. It is a defense against not only our own vulnerability but also our complicity in creating poverty.

If we took back this projection, we would stop denying that each of us plays a role in creating poverty—by our way of living, by our indifference, by our labeling them "poor" as if that is who they are, by our choice not to have them as neighbors and get to know them. Part of the tax reduction debate is the belief that we are wasting money on "those people." It is not that the people we project onto do not have some of the qualities we see; it is that the meaning we give to what we see—in this case, the label and categorization—is just projection. It's the same with the unemployed, with broken homes and broken-down neighborhoods, youth on the street, and all the other symptoms we live with.

In our philanthropy, this mind-set that the "other" is the problem means that we need to wait for them to change before the change we want in the world can come to pass. And until they change, we need to stay distant and contain them. This diverts us from the realization that we have the means, the tools, the thinking to create a world we want to inhabit, and to do it for all. If we saw others as another aspect of ourselves, we would welcome them into our midst. We would let them know that they belong, that they are neighbors, with all their complexity.

• • •

To continue, as a community, to focus on the needs and deficiencies of the most vulnerable is not an act of hospitality. It substitutes labeling for welcoming. It is isolating in that they become a special category of people, defined by what they cannot do. This isolates the most vulnerable. Despite our care for them, we do not welcome them into our midst; we service them. They become objects. This may be why it is easier to raise money for suffering in distant places or to celebrate the history of slavery's end than it is to raise money for our neighbors on the margin who are six blocks away. Their proximity stands in the way of our compassion. An example: In Cincinnati we have spent $110 million to construct a magnificent Freedom Center to celebrate the end of slavery. Six blocks away we have citizens living in very difficult conditions—and there is great reluctance to see the relationship between the two. We are willing to acclaim the victories of the past; yet, caught in our projection onto the poor, we sustain a colonial attitude toward the suffering of people down the street.

To be even more specific about projection, it shows up in communities through the conversations that focus on any of the needs, problems, and diagnostic categories through which we label others. For example, we limit our future when we frame conversations in the following ways:

- Young people on the corner or out of school become "youth at risk."
- People who served their time in jail become "ex-offenders."
- People who live on the street become "homeless" or "vagrants."
- Those with physical or mental challenges become "handicapped" and "bipolar."
- Immigrants become "illegals."

And the list goes on based on the mood of the times.

This labeling, along with the services that flow out of it, is the "commercialization of needs" that John McKnight has written about. It becomes the justification for the fear-and-fault conversation that in turn justifies the context of retribution. Which in turn drives all the programs, expertise, and policy that we thought were going to make the difference.

Taking Back the Projection

When we stay isolated, there is no way to take back the communal projection. No amount of inner work or healing as individuals will be powerful. Projection sustains itself in the absence of relatedness, in a life or workplace where we have no sense of belonging. It cannot be taken back by acting alone. It does not disappear no matter how much data is presented, no matter how much moral suasion or guilt we try to produce. "Why can't we all just get along?" was a poignant plea, but it had no power to join us together.

Communal transformation, taking back our collective projections, occurs when people connect with those who were previously strangers, and when we invite people into conversations that ask them to act as creators or owners of community. It occurs when we become related in a new way to those we are intending to help. This means we stop labeling others for their deficiencies and focus on their gifts.

Example: Elementz

One example of a place where youth are valued rather than labeled is a center in Cincinnati named Elementz. A group of young people have created a hip-hop–oriented urban arts center where fourteen- to twenty-four-year-olds can spend three nights a week learning about writing, performing, disc jockeying, and producing hip-hop music. Their music. They also learn about graffiti as an art form and break dancing as a form of entertainment. Elementz takes the very things that bother many adults—the music, the dancing, the graffiti—and treats them as gifts. This is not a recreation center; it is a learning space where youth have to attend programs in order to be in the building.

Elementz was conceived by young people, and young people run it, so that when kids from the street walk into the building, they see a reflection of themselves and know they are welcome. The staff of the place are not professionally trained "youth workers"; they are young people two steps further down the road who have made a commitment and sacrifice to care for those coming behind them.

The goal of Elementz is not specifically to provide careers in these entertainment fields—that would be making a promise that is unreal. The goal is to give to young people an experience of what they can create, a sense of the value they have inside themselves. The ultimate goal is to offer them a new possibility for their lives. It also serves to overcome the isolation of urban youth. When they walk in the door for the first time, if you ask them how many adults in their life have their best interest at heart, their answer is one or two. If you ask them the same question after they have participated in Elementz for six months, the answer is four to five. This experience makes the difference. When they are less isolated, and have adults interested in their well-being, they have the will to retreat from the street culture and begin to construct a more productive life for themselves.

Nothing guarantees that a young person will see a new possibility, but we can create the conditions where that choice is more likely. The transformation we seek occurs when these two conditions are created: when we produce deeper relatedness across boundaries, and when we create new conversations that focus on the gifts and capacities of others.

These conditions allow us to focus on our connectedness rather than on our differences. We no longer need to take our identity from being right about "them" or from continuing to see "them" as individuals with needs or as people somehow less than us. It puts an end to our need to declare victory. The differences, instead of being problems to solve, become a source of vitality, a gift. In the language of community transformation, this is what it means to be accountable. At these moments, we become owners, with the free will capable of creating the world we want to inhabit. We become citizens.

CHAPTER 6

The Inversion into Citizen

Choosing to be accountable for the whole, creating a context of hospitality and collective possibility, acting to bring the gifts of those on the margin into the center—these are some of the ways we begin to create a community of citizens. To reclaim our citizenship is to be accountable, and this comes from the inversion of what is cause and what is effect. When we are open to thinking along the lines that citizens create leaders, that children create parents, and that the audience creates the performance, we create the conditions for widespread accountability and the commitment that emerges from it. This inversion may not be the whole truth, but it is useful.

• • •

If what holds the possibility of an alternative future for our community is our capacity to come fully into being as citizens, then we have to talk about this word *citizen*. Our definition here is that a citizen is one who is willing to be accountable for and committed to the well-being of the whole. That whole can be a city block, a workplace, a community, a nation, the earth. A citizen is one who produces the future, someone who does not wait, beg, or dream for the future.

The antithesis of being a citizen is being a consumer or a client, another idea that John McKnight has been so instructive about. Consumers give power away. They believe that their own needs can be best satisfied by the actions of others—whether those others are elected officials, top management, social service providers, or the shopping mall. Consumers also allow others to define their needs. If leaders and service providers are guilty of labeling or projecting onto others the "needs" to justify their own style of leadership or service they provide, consumers collude with them by accepting others' definition of their needs. This provider–consumer transaction is the breeding ground for entitlement, and it is unfriendly to our definition of citizen and the power inherent in that definition.

The Meaning of Citizenship

The conventional definition of citizenship is concerned with the act of voting and taking a vow to uphold the constitution and laws of a country. This is narrow and limiting. Too many organizations that are committed to sustaining democracy in the world and at home have this constrained view of citizenship. Citizenship is not about voting, or even about having a vote. To construe the essence of citizenship primarily as the right to vote reduces its power—as if voting ensures a democracy. It is certainly a feature of democracy, but as Fareed Zakaria points out in his book *The Future of Freedom*, the right to vote does not guarantee a civil society, or in our terms a restorative one.

When we think of citizens as just voters, we reduce them to being consumers of elected officials and leaders. We see this most vividly at election time, when candidates become products, issues become the message, and the campaign is a marketing and distribution system for the selling of the candidate. Great campaign managers are great marketers and product managers. Voters become target markets, demographics, whose most important role is to meet in focus groups to respond to the nuances of message. This is the power of the consumer, which is no power at all.

Through this lens, we can understand why so many people do not vote. They do not believe that their action can impact the future. It is partly a self-chosen stance and partly an expression of the helplessness that grows out of a retributive world. This way of thinking is not an excuse not to vote, but it does say that our work is to build the capacity of citizens to be accountable and to become creators of community.

• • •

We can see most clearly how we marginalize the real meaning of *citizen* when the word becomes politicized as part of the retributive debate. We argue over undocumented workers, immigration, and the rights of ex-felons—and even their children. We politicize the issue of English as the official language and building a new wall on the Rio Grande that we will have to tear down someday.

Citizenship as the willingness to build community gets displaced by isolationism in any form. It is not by accident that the loudest activists for finding and deporting undocumented workers are some of the leaders of the fear, oversight, safety, and security agenda. They are the key beneficiaries of the retributive society. If we want community, we have to be unwilling to allow citizenship to be co-opted in this way.

The idea of what it means to be a citizen is too important and needs to be taken back to its more profound value. Citizenship is a state of being. It is a choice for activism and care. As a citizen you are someone who is willing to do the following:

- Hold yourself accountable for the well-being of the larger collective of which you are a part. Don't answer the question "What's in it for me?" When asked, simply say, "I don't know."

- Choose to own and exercise power rather than defer or delegate it to others. Set aside your wish for great leadership. You may be it. How enticing is that?

- Enter into a collective possibility that gives hospitable and restorative community its own sense of being.

- Acknowledge that community grows out of citizens' deciding to trust each other and cooperate to make this place better. Community is built not by specialized expertise or great leadership or improved services; it is built by great local people deciding to do something useful together.

- Attend to the gifts and capacities of all others, and act to bring the gifts of those on the margin into the center. Find a way to do this each time you meet. To understand our gifts, we need to hear about them from each other as a practice for ending a gathering. Citizenship is the knowledge that I have contributed something of value. I have to hear to believe it.

The Inversion of Cause

To create communities where citizens reclaim their power, we need to shift our beliefs about who is in charge and where power resides. We need to invert our thinking about what is cause and what is effect. This shift is what has the capacity to confront our entitlement and dependency.

Being powerful means that my experience, my discovery, even my pleasure are mine to create. This view has us see how audiences create performances, children create parents, students create teachers, and citizens create leaders.

> The chicken is the egg's way of reproducing itself.
>
> Peter Koestenbaum

It is not that these shifts of cause are necessarily true, but they give us power. In every case, it puts choice into our own hands instead of having us wait for the transformation of others to give us the future we desire. If our intention is to create the possibility of an alternative future, then we need a future formed by our own hands. A handcrafted future.

Inverting our thinking does not change the world, but it creates a condition where the shift in the world becomes possible. The shift starts with the inversion in our thinking. The step from thinking of ourselves as effect to thinking of ourselves as cause is the act of inversion that creates a culture of citizen accountability. This is the point on which accountability revolves.

A note: the cause-and-effect, Cartesian clockwork view of the world not only overstated the mechanical nature of the world but also put cause at the wrong end of the equation. Double indemnity.

This inversion challenges conventional wisdom that believes there is one right way. And by "inversion" I mean a real inversion: 180 degrees, not 179 degrees. This is not the time for compromise or balance. Inverting our thinking about cause and effect gives support to really challenge "the way things work." Again, I am not saying that this way of thinking is 100 percent accurate 100 percent of the time, but it can give added power to our way of being in community. The question to begin to reclaim our power as citizens is, "If you believed this to be true, in what ways would that make a difference, or change your actions?"

This means that the possibility of an alternative future centers on the question, "Have we chosen the present, or has it been handed to us?"

The default culture would have us believe that the past creates the future, that a change in individuals causes a change in organizations and community, and that people in authority create people in a subordinate position. That we are determined by everything aside from free will. That culture, history, genetics, organizations, and society drive our actions and our way of being.

All this is true, but the opposite is also true: that free will trumps genetics, culture, and parental upbringing.

The Utility of This Inversion

The first inversion I ran into years ago was the thought that the inmates run the prison. I was skeptical until I worked with some corrections people, who said there is truth in this. Here are some implications of switching our thinking this way:

Inversion: The audience creates the performance.

Implications: Redesign the audience experience. Stop putting so much energy into the talent and message of those on stage. Limit PowerPoint presentations to four slides. Peter Brook immersed the stage in the center of the audience; John Cage held concerts where the rumbling, coughing sounds of the audience *were the show*. When we meet, make it possible for the audience to be engaged with one another. Every auditorium, almost every church, almost every conference room and classroom would be redesigned. Chairs would be mobile; the audience members would be able to see one another and know that no matter what occurred onstage, they would not be alone and would have the ability to get what they came for.

Inversion: The subordinate creates the boss.

Implications: Learning, development, and goal setting are in the hands of the subordinate. We would stop doing surveys about how people feel about their bosses, the results of which no one knows what to do with anyway. The attention would turn from the boss to peers, which is the relationship that produces the work.

Inversion: The child creates the parent.

Implications: Parents could sleep through the night. The conversation and industry of inculcating values and forcing consequences onto kids would quiet down. We would focus on the gifts, teachings, and blessings of the young instead of seeing them as problems to be managed. We would decide that the primary role of the parent is to discover who these strange little creatures we call children really are. We would listen to them instead of instructing and teaching them again and again. This would allow parents to relax their jaws and index fingers, a secondary health benefit.

Inversion: Citizens create their leaders.

Implications: Our dependency on leaders and our disappointment in them would go down. The media would have to change their thinking about lead stories. What citizens are doing to improve their community would no longer be human interest stories but actual news. The cost of elections would be reduced by 90 percent, for the question of whom we elect would be less critical. Candidates for elected office could be poor.

Above all, our leaders would be conveners, not role models and containers for our projections. More on this later.

Inversion: A room and a building are created by the way they are occupied.

Implications: We would be intentional about how we show up. We would spend time designing how we sit in the room, and not be mere consumers of the way the room was intended to be used, or dependent on what the custodians or the last group using the room had in mind.

We would redesign the physical space around us—rooms, hallways, reception areas—in a way that affirmed community, so that it had a welcoming feeling and gave the sense that you had come to the right place. Most of all, how we sit together would be a serious subject of discussion.

Inversion: The student creates the teacher and the learning.

Implications: Education would be designed more for learning than for teaching. This already occurs in many places under the heading of individualized learning. Montessori education has forever operated along these lines. The social contract in the classroom would be renegotiated toward a partnership between teacher and student. Students would set goals for themselves and be responsible for the learning of other students. Simple ideas, powerful ideas, still rare in practice. This would also find a resting place for standardized testing and the colonial drive for a core curriculum.

Inversion: Youth create adults.

Implications: Adultism would be confronted. Adults would decide to get interested in the experience of youth instead of always instructing them. When there were meetings and conferences about youth, the voices of youth would be central to the conversation. Youth would become a possibility, not a problem. If we really believed this, we would move our belief in the next generation from lip service to pervasive practice. The question we would ask of youth is "What is it that we do not understand about you?" This would be life changing, if we had the nerve.

Inversion: The listening creates the speaker.

Implications: Listening would be considered an action step. For most of us, listening is just waiting until we get a chance to speak. There might even be a period of silence between statements, and this silence would be experienced as part of the conversation, not dead space. The dark side of virtual communication is that there is little place for silence. If we were in the room together and you were quiet, we would wait. If we are in a Zoom call and you don't speak, we think it is a failure in technology.

Listening would drive our speaking. We would also learn what speaking into the listening of the room means. Fundamentally, we would treat the listening as more important than the speaking.

You get the point—the list could go on. In each case, when we invert our thinking, the focus of attention and effort gets redirected.

The power in these shifts is that they confront us with our own freedom in unexpected ways. It is out of this freedom, which all of us have ways of escaping, that community and authentic accountability are born. I will be an accountable possibility for only that which I have had a hand in creating, my life and community included.

The politics of this is that the inversion of cause refocuses my attention from that person in authority—leader, performer, parent, warden—to that person who together with others also holds the real power. Not to overdo this perspective, for leader, performer, parent, and warden are critical partners in community; it's just that they are not the primary or sole proprietors we have construed them to be. We will never eliminate our need for great leaders and people on the stage; we just cannot afford to put all our experience and future in their hands.

* * *

There is no need to argue about this idea of inversion, only to play with its utility. A given inversion may not be true, but it is useful in the way it gives us power to evoke the kind of citizen we have defined as crucial to a true community. People who work in the civic arena have a certain cynicism about citizens. For example, they talk about how hard it is to get parents involved in their child's school. About how few people show up at council and board meetings unless they are angry. About how such a small number of people are really active in their community. There is truth to this view. It is not just cynicism; it is pretty accurate observation. What restores community is to believe that we play a role in constructing this condition. It is not in the nature of people to be apathetic, entitled, complainers.

To state the issue simply, as long as we see leader as cause, we will produce passive, entitled citizens. We will put our attention, our training, and our resources wherever we think cause resides. When we see citizen as cause, then this will shift our attention and our wealth, and the energy and creativity that go with them.

This shift in thinking about cause and effect creates the belief that in each case, including our individual lives, choice and destiny replace accident and fate. No small thing.

A Word About Accountability

One cost of the retributive conversation is that it breeds entitlement. Entitlement is essentially the conversation, "What's in it for me?" It expresses a consumer mentality, and the economist tells us that only what is scarce has value. Entitlement is the outcome of a patriarchal culture, which I have discussed too often in other books. But for this discussion, I'll simply say that if we create a context of fear, fault, and retribution, then we will focus on protecting ourselves, which plants the seed of entitlement.

The cost of entitlement is that it is an escape from accountability and soft on commitment. What is interesting is that the existing public conversation claims to be tough on accountability, but the language of accountability as it is used in a retributive context is code for "control." High-control systems are unbearably soft on accountability. They keep screaming for tighter controls, new laws, and bigger systems, but in the scream, they expose their weakness.

The weakness in the dominant view of accountability is that it thinks people can be *held* accountable. That we can force people to be accountable. Despite the fact that it sells easily, it is an illusion to believe that retribution, incentives, legislation, new standards, and tough consequences will cause accountability.

This illusion is what creates entitlement—and worse, it drives us apart; it does not bring us together. It turns neighbor against neighbor. It denies that we are our brother's keeper. Every colonial and autocratic regime rises to power by turning citizens against each other. To control a culture, fear has to be sold. Through the central control of the media. By the crisis-based story line of journalism. Community is built by the stories of success. Community is undermined by finding who was at fault. This is the methodology of empire.

To see our conventional thinking about accountability at work, notice the conversations that dominate our meetings and gatherings. We spend time talking about people not in the room. If not that, our gatherings are designed to sell, change, persuade, and influence others, as if their change will help us reach our goals. These conversations do not produce power; they consume it.

Chosen Accountability, Commitment, and the Use of Force

Commitment and accountability are forever paired with each other and linked with creating community. None exists without the others. Accountability is the willingness to care for the well-being of the whole; commitment is the willingness to make a promise with no expectation of return.

The economist would say this smacks of altruism, and so be it. What community requires is a promise devoid of barter and not conditional on another's action. Without that, we are constantly in the position of reacting to the choices of others. Which means that our commitment is conditional. This is barter, not commitment.

The cost of constantly reacting to the choices of others is increased cynicism and helplessness. The ultimate cost of cynicism and helplessness is that we resort to the use of force. In this way, the barter mentality that dominates our culture proliferates force. Not necessarily violence, but the belief that for anything to change, we must mandate or use coercion.

The use of force is an end product of retribution, which rejects altruism and a promise made for its own sake. It rejects the idea that virtue is its own reward.

Commitment is the antithesis of entitlement and barter. Unconditional commitment with no thought to "What's in it for me?" is the emotional and relational essence of community. It is what some call integrity, fidelity, honoring your word.

Commitment is to choose a path for its own sake. This is the essence of power. Mother Teresa got this. When asked why she worked with people one at a time rather than caring more about having impact on a larger scale, she replied, "I was called by faith, not by results." If you want to join the chorus arguing with Mother Teresa, be my guest.

CHAPTER 7

The Transforming Community

Conventional thinking about communal transformation *believes that focusing on large systems, better leaders, clearer goals, and more controls is essential, and that emphasizing speed and scale is critical. The conventional belief is that individual transformation leads to communal transformation. Our explorations to this point lead instead to the understanding that transformation occurs when we focus on the structure of how we gather and the context in which the gatherings take place; when we work hard on getting the questions right; when we choose depth over speed and relatedness over scale. We also believe that problem solving can make things better but cannot change the nature of things.*

Community transformation calls for citizenship that shifts the context from a place of fear and fault, law and oversight, corporation and "systems," and preoccupation with leadership to one of gifts, generosity, and abundance; social fabric and chosen accountability; and associational life and the engagement of citizens. These shifts occur as citizens face each other in conversations of ownership and possibility. To be more specific, leaders are held to three tasks: to shift the context within which people gather, name the debate through powerful questions, and listen rather than advocate, defend, or provide answers.

• • •

The mind-set that we can program and problem-solve our way into a vision does not take into account the complexity and relational nature of community. It undervalues the importance of context and the linguistic, conversational nature of community. If we want to see a change in our communities, we must let go of the conventional or received wisdom about how change occurs. This means we reject or at least seriously question the beliefs that communal change will occur in the following circumstances:

- **We count on an aggregation of individual changes.** We have seen this in attempts by large organizations trying to change their culture through large-scale trainings and change efforts. Communities initiate large-scale dialogue programs and book clubs where many are simultaneously reading the same book. No matter how well intentioned, these efforts largely fall short of their goals. Why? Because individual lives are touched, but the organizational culture and the community are unmoved.

  What's missing is that these efforts do not recognize that there is such a thing as a collective body. A community benefits from shifts in individual consciousness, but needs a communal connectedness as well, a communal structure of belonging that produces the foundation for the whole system to move. This is why it is so frustrating to create high performance and consciousness in individuals and in individual institutions and then find that they have so little impact on the social capital or fabric of the community.

- **We think in terms of scale and speed.** As David Bornstein has so clearly pointed out, something shifts on a large scale only after a long period of small steps, organized around small groups patient enough to learn and experiment and learn again. Speed and scale are the arguments against what individual and communal transformation requires. They are a hallmark of the corporate mind-set. When we demand more speed and scale, we are making a coded argument against anything important being any different.

- **We stay focused on large systems and top leaders to implement better problem solving, clearer goals and vision, and better control of the process.** Large-system change is useful, but transforming action is always local, customized, unfolding, and emergent. The role of leaders is not to be better role models or to drive change;

their role is to create the structures and experiences that bring citizens together to identify and solve their own issues.

Communal transformation does occur when we accept the following beliefs:

- **We focus on the structure of how we gather and the context in which our gatherings take place.** Collective change occurs when individuals and small diverse groups engage one another in the presence of many others doing the same. It comes from the knowledge that what is occurring in one space is similarly happening in other spaces, especially ones where I do not know what they are doing. This is the value of a network, or even a network of networks, which is today's version of a social movement. In paying attention to the structure and context of our gatherings, we declare our faith in restoration. All this needs to be followed up with the usual actions and problem solving, but it is in those moments when citizens engage one another, in communion with and in the witness of others, that something collective shifts.

  Keeping this focus is especially critical when individuals and institutions meet across boundaries. The key is to structure a way of crossing boundaries so that people become connected to those they are not used to being in the room with. Every gathering, in its composition and in its structure, has to be an example of the future we want to create. If this is achieved in this gathering, then that future has occurred today and there is nothing to wait for. Pretty Zen.

- **We work hard on getting the questions right.** This begins by realizing that the questions themselves are important, more important than the answers. The primary questions for community transformation are "How do we choose to be together?" and "What do we want to create together?" These are different from the primary questions for individual transformation, which are "How do I choose to be in whatever setting I find myself in?" and "What am I called to do in this world?"

- **We choose depth over speed and relatedness over scale.** The question "What do we want to create together?" is deceptively complicated. It implies a long journey crossing social, class, and institutional boundaries. Depth takes time and the willingness to engage. Belonging requires the courage to set aside our usual notions of action and of measuring success by the numbers touched. It also means that while we keep our own point of view, we leave our self-interest at the door and show up to learn rather than to advocate. These are the conditions whereby we find new places where we belong.

Choosing Possibility over Problem Solving

Creating a future is different from defining a future. If our goal is to build social capital and to change the way that citizens are engaged with each other, then we have to shift our thinking about the roles that traditional strategy and problem solving take. We talked earlier about valuing gifts and possibility over needs and problems. Now we can be more detailed about what this looks like.

Our typical way of creating a future is by specifying the vision and the goals and then defining a blueprint to achieve them. This is called a destination strategy for solving problems. Here are the strategic elements of traditional problem solving:

- **Identify a need.** Find a problem, need, or deficiency that we want to fix or improve.

- **Study and analyze the need.** Do research, assemble facts, survey people, and organize survey results and data to make a compelling case for change.

- **Search for solutions.** Brainstorm alternatives. Benchmark where others have solved this deficiency. Bring in experts, consultants, academics, former leaders, and former public officials to provide good approaches.

- **Establish goals.** Set realistic and achievable goals, based on the vision. Define outcomes and narrow the effort toward results that can be achieved; the quicker and lower the cost the better. Search for the low-hanging fruit. Maybe initiate a pilot project to prove the viability of the strategy. Laminate the vision, mission, and goals to demonstrate the permanence of this intention.

- **Bring others on board.** Sell to key leaders, meet with citizens to define the effort and name the playing field. Enlist organizations and individuals to create an alliance for change. Publicize the burning platform and stress the urgency and the need for quick results. Give wide distribution to the laminate.

- **Implement.** Launch the program and drive it forward. Stay on message, and measure at frequent intervals. Hold people accountable for results, fulfilling promises, and showing outcomes. Declare to others how accountable we are.

- **Loop back.** When the world intervenes and creates a bump in the road, begin the problem solving anew, identifying what went wrong and who was responsible, and initiating a clear oversight process so that this will not happen again.

The essence of these classic problem-solving steps is the belief in a blueprint. We are all problem solvers, action oriented and results minded. It is illegal in this culture to leave a meeting without a to-do list. We want measurable outcomes and we want them now. And this all has such face validity that it seems foolish to argue in any way against it.

Also, this way of thinking does indeed work for many things, especially for the material world. It does not work well with human systems or when the desire is to create something out of nothing. We still believe that in building a community, we are in effect building and operating a clock. Once again, problem solving can make things better, but it cannot change the nature of things. This insight is at the center of all the thinking about complex adaptive systems, emergent design, and the organic and self-regulating nature of the universe.

The limitations of a clockwork strategy for the future can be seen in one of the most popular forms of community problem solving: creating a vision. Most communities have at some point described a vision for themselves—

these visions are developed as a way of defining the destination. (The new millennium was a great occasion for this. Now the horizon has shifted to 2030.) These types of visions have value in that they bring many people together for the sake of development, and they give form to the optimism we hold for ourselves. But they are limited in their power to transform because they assume that a defined destination can be reached in a linear path from where we are today.

Most visions are based on the belief that we know a lot about what constitutes an ideal or healthy community, which is true. There are many wonderful books that describe what a great community looks like. Jane Jacobs crystallized our thinking about the power of street life. Robert Putnam raised our consciousness about the centrality of social capital. John McKnight's work has built wide support for asset-based community development.

The challenge for community building is this: while visions, plans, and committed top leadership are important, even essential, no clear vision, nor detailed plan, nor committed group leaders have the power to bring this image of the future into existence without the continued engagement and involvement of citizens. In most instances, citizen engagement ends when the plan is in place. The implementation is put in the hands of the professionals. In concept, the master plan provides some parameters for development and the use of space, but in real life it usually is a call to let the arguing begin. For all its utility, it rarely builds interdependence or strengthens the social fabric of a place.

What brings a fresh future into being is citizens who are willing to self-organize. An alternative future needs the investment of citizens—leaders not in top positions—who are willing to pay the economic and emotional price that creating something really new requires.

Therefore, the challenge for every community is not so much to have a vision of what it wants to become, or a plan, or specific timetables. The real challenge is to discover and create the means for engaging citizens that brings a new possibility into being. To state it more precisely, what gives power to communal possibility is the imagination and authorship of citizens led through a process of engagement. This is an organic and relational process. This is what creates a structure of belonging. This is more critical than the vision and the plan.

Example: Covington

In Covington, Kentucky, several city institutions together chose to use this kind of community building as a way of developing a strategic plan for its civil servants and citizens. City Manager Jay Fossett; the head of the Center for Great Neighborhoods, Tom DiBello; and the head of the local business association, Gina Breyfogle, asked for help with a series of citizen gatherings to create the agenda for the city following the protocol suggested in this book. Under the leadership of Jeff Stec, a very talented local community builder, we invited the citizens of Covington to four public gatherings. Not to advise the leaders, but to define the priorities of the plan and to commit to making the strategic plan work. Five hundred people in a town of forty-four thousand showed up to do just this.

Each session had people meeting in small groups, working with people they did not know but with whom they shared a common interest. They answered open-ended questions, were asked to choose among priorities, and, in the final session, were asked for their commitment to bring this planning process into reality.

At the end of the process, the city had its strategic plan—and, more important, it had the commitment of a significant group of citizens signed up to make the plan work. Perhaps most important, they strengthened the fabric of their community in the process.

What creates an alternative future is acting on the belief that context, relatedness, and language are the point, and that traditional problem solving needs to be subordinated and postponed until context, relatedness, and language have shifted. In this thinking, problem solving becomes a means, not an end in itself.

We cannot problem-solve our way into fundamental change, or transformation, or community. To state it one more way: this is not an argument against problem solving; it is an assertion that the primary work is to shift the context and language and thinking about possibility within which problem solving takes place.

This shift requires us to change our idea of what constitutes action, so that what was once seen as a means to an end now is itself valued as action. Another key insight from Jim Keene, who has spent his life in the public arena, is that "perhaps the purpose of problems is to give us an excuse to come together."

Expanding Our Idea of Action

Of course, just coming together has to provide some movement toward the future. Every time we meet, we want to feel that we have moved the action forward. Community has a purpose beyond relationship: it has to create livelihood, raise a child, care for our health, embrace the vulnerable. To have these communal effects, we have to reconstruct our definition of action.

The question then is, what qualifies as action? Traditionally, in order to be satisfied that we have spent our time well when we are together, we want a strategy, a list of next steps and milestones, and then a combination of brick and mortar and the knowledge of who will be responsible for what. Any change in the world will, in fact, need this kind of action. To say, however, that this is all that counts as action is too narrow.

If we are to value building social fabric and belonging as much as budgets, timetables, and bricks and mortar, we need to consider action in a broader way. For example:

> Would a meeting be worthwhile if we simply strengthened our relationship?
>
> Would a meeting be worthwhile if we learned something of value?
>
> Suppose in a meeting we simply stated our requests of each other and what we were willing to offer each other. Would that justify our time together?
>
> Or, in a gathering, what if we only discussed the gifts we wanted to bring to bear on the concern that brought us together. Would that be an outcome of value?
>
> Suppose we spent the time agreeing on what matters to us?

Saying yes to these questions opens and broadens the spectrum of what constitutes action, and this is the point. Relatedness, learning, requests, intentions, offers of gifts, agreements on what matters are outcomes as valuable as agreements and next steps.

It is not that we are gathering just for the sake of gathering. Or gathering to get to know each other. We come together for an exchange of value and to experience how relatedness, gifts, learning, and generosity are valuable to community. When we name these as outcomes, we're able to experience completion for the investment we made without having to leave with a list for the future.

Without these elements of connection, the traditional tasks lose their urgency and have to be constantly incentivized to be sustained. With this expanded notion of action, we can bring visioning, problem solving, and clearly defined outcomes into the room—and in fact we need them to sustain us. People will meet to learn and connect for only so long, and then they need a task. In addition to finding each other and having new conversations with people we are not used to talking to (at least in this way), it also helps to produce a physical thing. Clean something up, make a meal, start a community garden, walk some dogs, ask a neighbor if they are lonely. The practical becomes an excuse to be together, which is needed to sustain belonging over time.

PART TWO

The Alchemy
of Belonging

Certain properties of collective transformation create the conditions for greater
belonging and stronger social fabric. Not
that transformation can be reduced to a recipe or set of
steps, but its properties can be seen as a combination
of ingredients that give it a more concrete structure.
Our attempt to convert lead into gold, as it was for
the original alchemists, is part working with the right
properties and part an act of faith and spirit.

> To gain the
> kingdom of heaven
> is to hear what is
> not said, to see
> what cannot be
> seen, and to know
> the unknowable.
>
> Hawaiian Queen Liliuokalani
> to her daughter, after she
> saw the end of her monarchy

Up to this point, we have said that transformation
occurs when we shift context, value possibility, and shift
language, all of which produce a sense of belonging. We
can now be specific about the means for making this happen. The following
"pattern language," to borrow Christopher Alexander's term, when brought
into a context of caring for the whole, can produce a new future:

Leadership is convening.

The small group is the unit of transformation.

Questions are more transforming than answers.

Six conversations materialize belonging.

Hospitality, the welcoming of strangers, is central.

Physical and social space support belonging.

These provide the framework for the discussion of a methodology that puts the ideas from part 1 into practice.

CHAPTER 8

Leadership Is Convening

This is not an argument against leaders or leadership, only a desire to change the nature of our thinking about leadership. Communal transformation requires a certain kind of leadership, one that creates conditions where context shifts in the following ways:

- *From a place of fear and fault to one of gifts, generosity, and abundance*
- *From a belief in more laws and oversight to a belief in social fabric and chosen accountability*
- *From institutions, corporations, and systems as central, to associational life as central*
- *From a focus on leaders to a focus on citizens*
- *From problems to possibility*

For this shift in context to occur, we need leadership that supports a restorative path. Restoration calls for us to deglamorize leadership and consider it a quality that exists in all human beings. We need to simplify leadership and construct it so that it is infinitely and universally available. We need to end our search for better leaders. We have enough.

• • •

In communal transformation, leadership is about intention, convening, valuing relatedness, and presenting choices. It is not a personality characteristic or a matter of style, and therefore it requires nothing more than what all of us already have.

This means we can stop looking for leadership as though it were scarce or lost or had to be trained into us by experts. If our traditional form of leadership has been studied for so long, written about with such admiration, defined by so many, worshipped by so few, and the cause of so much disappointment, maybe doing more of all that is not productive. The search for great leadership is a prime example of how we too often take something that does not work and try harder at it.

I have written elsewhere about reconstructing *leader* as social architect. Not leader as special person, but leader as a citizen willing to do those things that have the capacity to initiate something new in the world. In this way, leader belongs right up there with cook, carpenter, artist, hair stylist, and landscape designer. It is a capacity that can be learned by all of us, with a small amount of teaching and an agreement to practice. The ultimate do-it-yourself movement.

Community building requires a concept of the leader as one who designs experiences for others—experiences that in themselves are examples of our desired future. *Experiences* here refers to the way people in the room interact with each other. The experiences we create need to be designed in such a way that relatedness, accountability, and commitment are every moment available, experienced, and demonstrated. David Isaacs of the World Café calls this "relational leadership."

This concept of leadership means that in addition to embracing their own humanity, which is the work of every person, the core task of leaders is to create the conditions for civic or institutional engagement. They do this through the power they have to name the debate and to design gatherings.

We use the term *gathering* because the word has different associations from what we think of when we say "meeting." Most people do not even like meetings, and for good reason. They are frequently designed to explain, defend, express opinions, persuade, set more goals, and define steps—the result of which is to produce more of what currently exists. These kinds of meetings either review the past or embody the belief that better planning, better managing, or more measurement and prediction can create an alternative future. So the word *gathering* is intended to distinguish what we are talking about here, something with more significance than the common sense of *meeting.*

Engagement Is the Point

Leadership begins with understanding that every gathering is an opportunity to deepen accountability and commitment through engagement. It doesn't matter what the stated purpose of the gathering is.

Each gathering serves two functions: to address its stated purpose, its business issues; and to be an occasion for each person to decide to become engaged as an owner. The leader's task is to structure the place and experience of these occasions to move the culture toward shared ownership.

This is very different from the conventional belief that the task of leadership is to set a vision, enroll others in it, and hold people accountable through measurements and reward. Consider how most current leadership trainings assert the following:

- Leader and top are essential. They are role models who need to possess a special set of personal skills.

- The task of the leader is to define the destination and the blueprint to get there.

- The leader's work is to bring others on board. Enroll, align, inspire.

- Leaders provide for the oversight, measurement, and training needed (as defined by leaders).

Each of these beliefs elevates leaders as an elite group, singularly worthy of special development, coaching, and incentives. All of these beliefs have face validity, and they have unintended consequences. When we are dissatisfied with a leader, we simply try harder to find a new one who will perform more perfectly in the very way that led to our last disappointment. This creates a burden of isolation, entitlement, and passivity that our communities cannot afford to carry.

The world does not need leaders to better define issues or to orchestrate better planning or project management. What it needs is for the issues and the plans to have more of an impact, and that comes from citizen accountability and commitment. Engagement is the means through which there can be a shift in caring for the well-being of the whole, and the task of leader as convener is to produce that engagement.

The Art of Convening

In this way of thinking, we hold leadership to three tasks:

- Create a context that nurtures an alternative future, one based on gifts, generosity, accountability, and commitment.
- Initiate and convene conversations that shift people's experience, which occurs through the way people are brought together and the nature of the questions used to engage them.
- Listen and pay attention. Be able to say "I don't know."

Convening leaders create and manage the social space within which citizens become deeply engaged and discover that it is in their power to resolve something or at least move the action forward. Engagement, and the accountability that grows out of it, occurs when we ask people to be in charge of their own experience and act on the well-being of the whole. Leaders do this by naming a new context and convening people into new conversations through questions that demand personal investment. This is what triggers the choice to be accountable for those things over which we can have power, even though we may have no control.

• • •

In addition to convening and naming the question, we add listening to the critical role of leadership. Listening may be the single most powerful action the leader can take. Leaders will always be under pressure to speak, but if building social fabric is important, and sustained transformation is the goal, then listening becomes the greater service.

This kind of leadership—convening, naming the question, and listening—is restorative and produces energy rather than consumes it. It is leadership that creates accountability as it confronts people with their freedom. In this way, engagement-centered leaders bring kitchen-table and street-corner democracy into being.

Example: Findley House

Seven Hills is a neighborhood center in the West End of Cincinnati. One of its locations is called Findley House, and a project there illustrates the power of engagement-centered listening. The story starts when four "leaders" were asked to work with a group of urban youths. The essence of the story is that they resisted the temptation to be helpful.

Joan and Michael Hoxsey and Geralyn and Tom Sparough were four white, overeducated adults when they first met with a dozen streetwise African American youths in what began as an intervention to help the youths, including a full curriculum on what these young men "ought" to learn about relationships.

Shortly into the effort, the Hoxseys and Sparoughs realized that to make any difference in the young men's lives, the adults had to try to understand who these young people were. So they threw out the curriculum and decided to simply hang out with the youths. They listened two nights a week for eight months. The listening was hard, the language was hard, the stories were heartbreaking.

At first it seemed the young men were unreachable, and any attempt to "help" would be futile. Then, at some point the adults' listening made a difference. The adults and the young people began to trust one another. As one young man put it, "The reason I respect you so much is because you may be the only people who really listen. Everyone wanted to tell us to 'pull up our pants' and tell us how to live." Something valuable was built, and in the end the "things" the adults wanted to teach about relationships were taught by simply changing the nature of the conversation.

In this same facility, there were two other programs for the youth started at the same time: GED training and computer skills training. Both of these programs had something in mind for the young men, something the leadership knew was best for them. By the end of this part of the program, the youths simply stopped showing up. Operating under the traditional ideas of good leadership, the GED program and the computer training program were gone. The youths rejected that kind of help.

Even when the program that brought the youths and the Hoxseys and Sparoughs together ended, these adults and youths continued to meet, and they managed to produce a movie about the crucible of choices facing young urban people. What turned out to be sustainable and durable over time was the program of listening and valuing run by the Hoxseys and Sparoughs, whom the youths decided to trust. And, eight years later, there is another movie, and those of the original group still around are still connected.

One of the challenges facing relational approaches such as this is that they do not measure well. If we were to take a conventional approach to measuring these efforts, we would look for computer skill improvement and how many youths got their GED diplomas. The report would give low marks to the easily measured expected outcomes. We would probably conclude that the youths were not ready to learn. We would not consider the computer and GED efforts a failure in leadership—that would be too strong an indictment of our current thinking.

The social outcomes of the Hoxseys and Sparoughs' work would most likely not be valued by the assessment at all, nor would their leadership style show up as a positive factor. Conventional measures would miss the essence of the humanity and restraint that led to transformation that took the form of a group of young African Americans finding four white people, in positions of leadership, whom they could trust.

The Convening Capacity of Elected Officials

Elected officials are a special case in how we think about leadership and the art of convening. We have put elected officials in a difficult role. We distort them into service providers and suppliers. We relate to them as if we are consumers, not citizens. We want them to solve *for* us those issues that we should be solving for ourselves.

The customer model, in which elected officials exist to satisfy citizen demands, is a disservice to community, even though citizens love it. Elected officials are partners with citizens, not suppliers. The most useful role that elected officials can perform is to bring citizens together. They have this convening capacity like no one else in a city, but it is seriously underutilized. If elected officials take on this role as their primary one, we may still occasionally request that they pass some legislation or ordinance that serves us, but this should be the exception. If we continue to define elected officials primarily as legislators, then we are going to have to endure the results of their productivity.

Example: Cold Spring

Mark Stoeber was the mayor of Cold Spring, Kentucky, a small and mostly residential town. At some point he realized that the citizen complaints he was getting did not need an elected official to resolve. For example, he was getting complaints in one neighborhood about someone's dog. Mark decided that the complaint about the dog was a symptom of the lack of connectedness among neighbors. With the dog's behavior as cover, he asked one citizen to host a meeting in her home with other neighbors. Neighbors showed up, including the dog owner, and an agreement was reached. The social fabric became a little stronger. The mayor moved on to other things.

A year later, Mark decided to take another step and invited about twenty community leaders into a conversation with city council members. They met in council chambers, but not in the usual configuration. In Cold Spring, as in most cities, the council sits on a platform and citizens sit in seats on a lower level. For this meeting, everyone sat in chairs in circles at the same level in the council room. They arranged themselves in groups to sit with people they knew the least, and talked about some of the questions we are discussing here: crossroads facing the town, the major gifts of the town and its citizens, doubts about anything really shifting, a look at the future demands facing the town, and what commitment they had to participate in engaging more people to develop the possibility called Cold Spring.

This was a small but symbolic beginning for an elected official deciding that the future economic development and quality of life of the town were dependent on the quality of relatedness of its citizens and its ability to bring those on the margin into the center.

Local government has two primary responsibilities. One is to sustain and improve the infrastructure of its community: roads, traffic, transportation, public safety, code enforcement, economic development, master planning, environment, and more. City managers and civil servants are well trained to do this and mostly do an excellent job at it.

The other role of local government is to build the social fabric of the community. Officials are in a key position to engage citizens in the well-being of the city. The challenge in doing this is intensified by the structures they most often use to do it. The typical forms of engagement are city council meetings, public hearings, neighborhood summits, town hall meetings, and any variety of speaking engagements and special events that they attend.

There is nothing in the current structure of these gatherings that encourages citizens to connect with each other or to be engaged as producers of the future. Citizens show up as critics and consumers.

For local government to build the social fabric and create the context for a restorative community, the form in which citizens are involved needs to change from a patriarchal, consumer model to a partnership model that takes advantage of the energizing power of the small group.

The idea that leadership is primarily about convening is a hard sell. It assaults the heroic projections we want to place on our leaders. We want to believe that leaders create followers. Especially when we choose the leaders. This idea requires us to take the parenting out of power. Leadership has the job of caring for the common good, for the well-being of all. No question of the special demands of this task. It is in the thinking and collective awareness of the leader that community often hinges. This is what we want to nudge.

CHAPTER 9

The Small Group Is
the Unit of Transformation

The future is created one room at a time, one gathering
at a time. Each gathering needs to become an example of the future
we want to create. This means that the small group is where transformation takes place. Large-scale transformation occurs when enough
small groups are aggregated to lead to a larger change. Small groups
have the most leverage when they meet as part of a larger gathering.
At these moments, citizens experience the intimacy of the small circle
and are simultaneously aware that they are part of a larger whole that
shares their concerns.

*The small group gains power with certain kinds of conversations.
To build community, we seek conversations where people show up
by invitation rather than mandate, and experience an intimate and
authentic relatedness. We have conversations where the focus is on
the communal possibility, and there is a shift in ownership of this place,
even though others are in charge. We structure these conversations so
that diversity of thinking and dissent are given space, commitments are
made without barter, and the gifts of each person and our community
are acknowledged and valued.*

• • •

Communal transformation takes its most visible form in
those moments when we gather. It is when groups of people are
in a room together that a shift in context is noticed, felt, and reinforced.

This means that each gathering takes on a special importance as a leading indicator of the future. Every meeting or special event is that place where context can be shifted, relatedness can be built, and new conversation can be introduced. The times that we gather are when we draw conclusions about what kind of community we live in.

We change the world one room at a time. This room, today, becomes an example of the future we want to inhabit. There is no need to wait for the future. Creating the experience of belonging in the room we are in at the moment becomes the point, namely that the way we structure the assembly of peers and leaders is as critical as the issue or concerns we come together to address.

One conventional structure for meeting is described in *Robert's Rules of Order*. It is good at efficiency and containing conflict; it is also good at dampening energy. Even when *Robert's Rules* do not apply, which is most of the time, our meetings typically pay primary attention to explanation, persuasion, and problem solving, rather than engagement, and in this way they also drain our aliveness. For community building, we want to give as much or more attention to that which creates energy as we give to the content, which usually exhausts energy.

Creating energy is critical, for in our gatherings we have the most control and influence over shifting the context and public conversation. It is true that other factors, such as the media message and the policy stance of public figures, make a difference. The media has a large impact on the narrative of our community and our experience of it. Public policy can make what we do easier or more difficult. However, most citizens who want an alternative future, including some of the community's leaders, have little short-term control over these factors. When there is a shift in the way citizens listen and speak, however, eventually there will be a shift in the context spoken by the media and the stance of public figures.

Therefore, like it or not, the way we design our gatherings is the only way we can bring into existence the possibility of authentic community. Everything that occurs outside the room we are in at the moment is an abstraction and leads us into conversations of complaint and wishful thinking. There is no power in the complaint, no power in more explanations or talking about who else should be in the room. These conversations are a defense against citizen power and action.

The Power of the Small Group

All change includes work in one or more small groups, which is why we use the shorthand sentence "The small group is the unit of transformation." The small group is the structure that allows every voice to be heard. It is in groups of three to twelve that intimacy is created. This intimate conversation makes the process personal. It provides the structure that enables people to overcome isolation and experience a sense of belonging. Even though we may be in a room filled with a large number of people we will never meet, by having made intimate contact with a handful of people in our small group work, we are brought into connection with all others.

The small group is therefore the bridge between our own individual existence and the larger community. In the small group discussion, we discover that our own concerns are more universal than we imagined. This discovery that we are not alone, that others can at least understand what is on our mind, if not agree with us, is what creates the feeling of belonging. When this occurs in the same place and time, in the presence of a larger community, the collective possibility begins to take form and have legs. The small group, three of us talking in a room full of other small groups talking, is a close-at-hand example of the larger life and world we want to inhabit. It is evidence in the moment that change is possible.

The power of the small group cannot be overemphasized. Something almost mystical, certainly mysterious, occurs when citizens sit in a small group, for they often become more authentic and personal with each other there than in other settings. Designing small group conversations (more about that later) is so simple that it rarely receives the attention and importance it deserves.

The small group also offers a self-correcting quality when things are not going well. There are always times in any gathering when we become stuck. Energy is low, perhaps there is anger or cynicism in the room, or simply confusion, and we are unsure what to do. The best path in nearly every situation is to put our faith in citizens to identify and name what is occurring. Simply request people to form small groups of three or four and ask them to discuss what is going on and report back in ten minutes. This request need not be sophisticated. Simply say, "Form small groups of four and talk about how this meeting is going and to what extent we are getting what we came for."

In doing this, we ask the community to take responsibility for the success of this gathering and express faith in their goodwill, even if they are frustrated with what is happening. This act is a way of shifting power and accountability from leader to citizens; and in most cases, citizens will identify what needs to occur to get the action back on track. Doing this is an acknowledgment that critical wisdom resides in the community.

The point is that every large group meeting needs to use small groups to create connection and move the action forward. As obvious as this might seem, it amazes me how many events and gatherings do not do it. How many conferences, summits, and events have we attended where the small group discussion is relegated to the breaks and thereby left to chance?

The Role of the Large Group

In gatherings where there are more than twenty people in the room—which I am calling the large group—we need to move back and forth from the small group to the large group. The same if there are a thousand in the room. There have to be moments when the whole room hears individual voices and what other small groups are speaking about. Holding to the metaphorical meaning of "the room as a microcosm of the universe," when people share with a larger group, they are sharing with the world.

These are the moments where individuals have an opportunity to stand for something. So, as a symbol of the larger purpose of the gathering, a person speaking to the whole literally needs to physically stand. As they "stand" for something for themselves, they are standing for the sake of all in the room. As each person stands, we ask their name so that they can be known for their stance.

A place of belonging is one where all voices have value, so we need to make sure that citizens' voices receive the same technological boost as leaders'. When people speak to the large group, their voices need to be amplified so that all can hear. Our belief in the importance of the voices of citizens hinges on what may seem like a secondary matter: the availability of a microphone for all who choose to speak.

Having a standing microphone for citizens that they have to walk to and even line up behind does not count. Most public meetings have leaders with their own mics and citizens traveling to a common mic. The geography of this disparity speaks volumes as to who is important (leaders) and therefore who has the future in their hands. Juanita Brown and David Isaacs have expressed the profound insight that every moment is a combination of methodology and metaphor. What may seem like a small procedural or technological matter is actually much more important than we have imagined because of its metaphorical message. The amplification of a human voice is a good example of this.

What has slowly dawned on me over time is that the outcome of small and large group experiences is primarily determined by a set of details that I thought were incidental, as in the example mentioned here: people standing when they speak, the voice amplified so that the sound of the citizen is as clear as the sound of a leader.

Another example: ask people making a powerful statement to the whole community to say it again slowly. They speak for all others who are silent, and in that way they speak for the whole. These can be sacred moments, and repetition honors this. One more detail along these lines: when people speak in a large group, they need to be acknowledged for the courage it took to speak out.

Most of this way of being in groups is part of the emerging but well-established methodology often called *large group interventions*. These were noted in the first chapter. The intent throughout this book is to bring what has been facilitator technique into standard, everyday leadership practice, and to underline the potential power of these practices.

A Couple of Role Models

Mike McCartney is a longtime leader in Hawaii. His commitment as part of his Democratic Party work is to change the nature of the political debate there. He has been tireless in his effort to reframe elected officials as servant leaders and shift the conversation from problems and partisanship to the well-being of the whole community. Another leader who understands this is Jimmy Toyama. He also was a leader in the party who held a wider vision of the role a political party can play in society. To say that its main purpose is to win elections is too small a purpose. Jimmy held a series of conferences to create the conversation of possibility for the Democratic Party. Participants held conversations of gifts, ownership, and commitment . . . in small groups, with those they knew least. So simple, but very different from the usual party meeting. Jimmy is no longer chair of the party, but still gives his life to building community in Hawaii.

Conversations That Count

To say that the future is dependent on having conversations we have not had before does not mean that *any* new conversation will make a difference. So what specific kinds of conversations can create the relatedness and accountability that are the heart of a restorative context?

To create a community of accountability and belonging, we seek conversations where the following is true:

> An intimate and authentic *relatedness* is experienced.
>
> The world is shifted through *invitation* rather than mandate.
>
> The focus is on the communal *possibility.*
>
> There is a shift in *ownership* of this place, even though others are in charge.
>
> Diversity of thinking and *dissent* are given space.
>
> *Commitments* are made without barter.
>
> The *gifts* of each person and our community are acknowledged and valued.

These are the specific conversations that are central to communal transformation. It is when we choose to speak of invitation, possibility, ownership, dissent, commitment, and gifts that transformation occurs. This is the speaking and listening that is the linguistic shift that changes the context through which community can be restored and traditional problem solving and development can make the difference.

There is a great deal written and practiced about creating new conversations, all of which is valuable and holds the same spirit as what will be offered here. Much of what is written is about handling difficult conversations in a way that builds relationships and holding crucial conversations that are important for the success of an organization. There has been for some time an important dialogue movement to help people understand their own mental models and listen more deeply as an act of inquiry.

The types of conversations offered here, and explored in more depth in the next three chapters, are a little different in that they are aimed at building community, whereas many of the others are primarily aimed at individual development or improving relationships. Plus these community-building conversations are pointedly designed to confront the issue of accountability and commitment. That aside, all the movements toward shifting conversation are extremely valuable, and all serve to change the world in a positive way.

CHAPTER 10

Questions Are More
Transforming Than Answers

We can now be specific about defining the conversations that create trust, accountability, and connection. The essence of a productive community. The traditional conversations that seek to explain, study, analyze, define tools, and express the desire to change others are interesting but not powerful. They actually are forms of wanting to maintain control. If we adhere to them, they become a limitation to the future, not a pathway.

The future is brought into the present when citizens engage each other through questions of possibility, commitment, dissent, and gifts. Questions open the door to the future and are more powerful than answers in that they demand engagement. Engagement is what creates accountability. How we frame the questions is decisive. They need to be ambiguous, personal, and stressful. The way we introduce the questions also matters. We name the distinction the question addresses by stating what is different and unique about this conversation. We give permission for unpopular answers and inoculate people against advice and help. Advice is replaced by curiosity.

• • •

The major theme here, that transformation and restoration occur through the power of language and how we speak and listen to each other, is rather abstract. Nice theory, but operationally how does this occur? What is the means to achieve the full impact of this idea?

We begin by realizing, at a basic level, that we need a new conversation. Some will say we are already having these conversations. Maybe, but even if ownership, dissent, gifts, commitment, and possibility are on the agenda, they are rarely pursued in a way that causes a real shift. We need to identify a way to hold these conversations so that the chance of creating something new increases, so that they have the quality of aliveness we seek.

The conversation is not so much about the future for the community but is the future itself. A parallel way to think of this is to consider the meaning of a yoga practice. Anyone beginning yoga struggles with the postures and cannot help but feel inadequate, have doubts about their body, and think the purpose of the practice is the core strength and flexibility it produces, or not. We are told—and sometimes get—that even the way we breathe can be a pathway to a better life.

All this is true, but the larger insight, the meta-goal, is to realize that "how you do the mat is how you do your life." That the practice of yoga itself is your life. Creating good postures, breathing, and flexibility are simply fringe benefits. It is your way of doing the practice itself that is the breakthrough, not some future moment in which a better state of being has been achieved. This way there is nothing to wait for, no future or objective measure of accomplishment to be attained.

The same with certain conversations. Holding them in a restorative context—one of possibility, generosity, and gifts, in relationship with others—is as much the transformation as any place that those conversations might lead you. The right small group conversation releases aliveness and intention into the community. This creates the condition where the symptoms and fragmentation and breakdown can be healed. It is only within this context and communal aliveness that our skill at problem solving will make the difference.

Conversations that evoke accountability and commitment can best be produced through deciding to value *questions* more than answers, by choosing to put as much thought into questions as we have traditionally given to answers.

The Construction of Questions

Questions are the essential tools of engagement. They are the means by which we are all confronted with our freedom. In this sense, if you want to change the context, find powerful questions.

Questions create the space for something new to emerge. Answers, especially those that respond to our need for quick results, while satisfying, shut down the discussion, and the future shuts down with them. Most leaders are well schooled in providing answers and remain rather indifferent and naive as far as the use of questions goes. How many PowerPoint presentations have you seen flooded with answers, blueprints, analyses, and proposals? How many have you seen presenting questions?

What makes us impatient with questions and hungry for answers is that we confuse exploring a question with talk that has no meaning—namely, opinions, positions, argument, analysis, explanation, and defense—talk that leaves us despairing about citizens coming together to create something. Questions that trigger opinions, argument, analysis, explanation, and defense have little power. It is significant that most of the meetings we go to, and the conversations we engage in, have these qualities. They may be interesting, but that is different than being powerful.

Powerful questions, as opposed to interesting questions, are those that, in the answering, produce accountability and commitment. They are questions that take us to statements that have power, simply in the saying. These statements are requests, offers, and declarations and expressions of forgiveness, confession, gratitude, and welcome, all of which are memorable and have transformative power.

Without strong questions, we collude with people who might attend a gathering and choose not to join in cocreating the value of the event. The point is that the nature of the questions we ask either keeps the existing system in place or brings an alternative future into the room. So I want to distinguish in more detail between questions that have little power and those that have great power.

A reminder: Questions alone are not enough. Context matters. The mind-set that people bring to the room matters. How people came to be in the room matters. The room itself matters. The social structure of how people talk to each other matters. The action of the leader/convener matters. But for this moment, let us stay with the questions.

> Questions are fateful. They determine destinations. They are the chamber through which destiny calls.
>
> Godwin Hlatshwayo

Questions with Little Power

The existing narrative is organized around a set of traditional questions that have little power to create an alternative future. These are the questions the world is constantly asking. It is understandable that we ask them, but they carry no power; and in the asking, each of these questions is an obstacle to addressing what has given rise to the question in the first place:

How do we get people to be more committed?

How do we get others to be more responsible?

How do we get people to come on board and to do the right thing?

How do we hold those people accountable?

How do we get others to buy in to our vision?

How do we get those people to change?

How much will it cost, and where do we get the money?

How do we negotiate for something better?

What new policy or legislation will move our interests forward?

Where is it working? Who has solved this elsewhere, and how do we import that knowledge?

How do we find and develop better leaders?

Why aren't those people in the room?

If we answer these questions directly, from the context from which they are asked, we are supporting the mind-set that an alternative future can be negotiated, mandated, engineered, and controlled into existence. They call us to try harder at what we have been doing. They also keep us apart and deepen our isolation.

The hidden agenda in these questions is to maintain dominance and to be right. They urge us to raise standards, measure more closely, and return to basics, purportedly to create accountability. They are not really about returning to basics; they are about returning to what got us here. These questions have no power; they only carry force.

All these questions preserve innocence for the one asking. They imply that the one asking knows and that other people are a problem to be solved. These are each an expression of reliance on the use of force to make a difference in the world. They occur when we lose faith in our own power and the power of our community.

Questions that are designed to change other people are the wrong questions. Wrong, not because they don't matter or are based on ill intent, but because they reinforce the problem-solving model. They are questions that are the cause of the very thing we are trying to shift: the fragmented and retributive nature of our communities. The conversations about standards, measures, and the change needed in others destroy relatedness, and it is in this way that they work against belonging and community.

These questions are also a response to the wish to create a predictable future. We want desperately to take uncertainty out of the future. But when we take uncertainty out, it is no longer the future. It is the present projected forward. Nothing new can come from the desire for a predictable tomorrow. The only way to make tomorrow predictable is to make it just like today. In fact, what distinguishes the future is its unpredictability and mystery.

Questions with Great Power

Achieving accountability and commitment entails the use of questions through which, in the act of answering them, we become cocreators of the world. Our answers to the questions do not matter. The questions have an impact even if the response is to refuse to answer them.

To state this more dramatically: powerful questions are the ones that cause you to become an actor as soon as you answer them or even reflect on them. You no longer have the luxury of being a spectator of whatever it is you are concerned about. Regardless of how you answer these questions, you are guilty. Guilty of being an actor and participant in this world. Not a pleasant thought, but the moment we accept the idea that we have created the world, we have the power to change it.

Powerful questions also express the reality that change, like life, is difficult and unpredictable. They open up the conversation—in contrast to questions that are, in a sense, answers in disguise. Answers in disguise narrow and control the dialogue, and thereby the future.

We can generalize what qualities define great questions, and this gives us the capacity not just to remember a list but also to create powerful questions of our own.

A great question has three qualities:

> **It is ambiguous.** There is no attempt to try to precisely define what is meant by the question. This requires each person to bring their own, individual meaning into the room.

> **It is personal.** All passion, commitment, and connection grow out of what is most personal. We need to create space for the personal.

> **It evokes anxiety.** All that matters makes us anxious. It is our wish to escape from anxiety that steals our aliveness. If there is no edge to the question, there is no power.

Questions themselves are an art form worthy of a lifetime of study. They are what transform the hour. Here are some questions that have the capacity to open the space for a different future:

> What is the commitment you hold that brought you into this room?

> Why was it important for you to show up today?

> What is the price you or others pay for being here today?

> How valuable do you plan for this effort to be?

> What is the crossroads you face at this stage of the game?

> What is the story you keep telling about the problems of this community?

> What are the gifts you hold that have not been brought fully into the world?

> What is your contribution to the very thing you complain about?

What is it about you or your team, group, or neighborhood that no one knows?

These questions have the capacity to move something forward, and we will explore them—and others—in more depth in the coming chapters. By answering these kinds of questions, we become more accountable, more committed, more vulnerable; and when we voice our answers to one another, we grow more intimate and connected. What binds all of these questions is that in the asking they invite us to be personal, disclosing, and vulnerable. These are the adhesives of belonging. We are more connected, even if we choose not to answer the question.

The Setup Is Everything

Once we have a question, there is a way of setting up the conversation that makes a big difference. Context is decisive at every level. If the conversation is not set up clearly and intentionally, the old conversation will occur. To initiate a new conversation, we have to give a reason for it, and we have to warn people against bringing forth the limitations of the old conversation—in other words, we must guard against solution finding and advice giving.

The setup is as important as the question, for it provides the context. As a reminder: the context we are creating space for is relatedness, accountability, gifts, and generosity. Being precise about the setup is an essential task of leadership. Without a clear setup, citizens will revert each and every time to the default conversation. The setup inoculates us against the power and habit of speaking into scarcity and dependency. It is so seductive to start talking about the need for more funding, the wish for better leadership, the power of the media, and how others need to change.

There are four elements to the setup:

- Name the distinctions.
- Give permission for unpopular answers.
- Avoid advice and replace it with curiosity.
- Ask lower-risk questions first.

Name Distinctions

Each question has a quality that distinguishes it from the default mind-set. Making this distinction clear is critical. For example, if we want to confront people's willingness to join us as owners of this gathering, we ask, "How valuable an experience do you *plan* to have in this event?" This is distinguished from the question "How valuable an experience do you *want* to have?" or "How valuable an experience do you *think* this will be?" The distinction between "plan" and "want" or "think" is the difference between choice and wishful thinking or expectations. *Wanting* to have a good experience does not mean we choose it. We can make a *prediction* about how valuable the experience will be, but this puts us in the position of waiting to see what the world will provide us.

There is no power in wanting or predicting; the power is in deciding. Even if we say that we plan for this experience to be of no value, we have taken the stance of ownership. What is so difficult to communicate is that ownership is more important than results. If I say that I plan for something to not be valuable, I have shown up as an owner, and that is what brings an alternative future into being. The instant I show up as an owner, I have reclaimed my full membership in this community.

To ask what kind of experience we *plan* to have places the ownership of that experience clearly in our own hands. The language of what we plan requires us to be accountable.

Every community-building question is about creating a powerful distinction, as in the ownership example, and every time, the distinction needs to be named. In every conversation the issue is the same: moving toward choice and accountability for the well-being of the whole. In the case of ownership, the distinction is between planning and wanting/predicting. If we are not aware of the distinction that makes the question powerful, we shouldn't use the question.

Give Permission for Unpopular Answers

When people are asked a question, they are conditioned to seek the right answer to feel good or to fit in for the sake of belonging. Encourage them to answer honestly, by naming possible unpopular answers and supporting their expression.

For example, on the ownership question, let them know that an answer that says they plan for this to be a very poor experience is a fine one. Literally say, "If you plan for this meeting to be a waste of time, give it a 1 on a 7-point scale, where 1 is yuck and 7 is wow. It is more important to declare where you are at this moment than for you to demonstrate optimism." All we care about is that people own their experience, not that the experience be a good one.

Create an Advice-Free Zone

We need to tell people not to be helpful. Trying to be helpful and giving advice are really ways to control others. Advice is a conversation stopper. In community building, we want to substitute curiosity for advice. No call to action. No asking what they are going to do about it. Do not tell people how you handled the same concern in the past. Do not ask questions that have advice hidden in them, such as "Have you ever thought of talking to the person directly?"

Often citizens will ask for advice. The request for advice is a way that people surrender their sovereignty. If we give in to this request, we have, in this small instance, affirmed their servitude, their belief that they do not have the capacity to create the world from their own resources; more important, we have supported their escape from their own freedom.

Advice, even if people ask for it, also subverts relatedness. Urge citizens to ask one another instead, "Why does that mean so much to you?" When they answer, ask the same question again, "And why does *that matter* so much to you?" This question—"Why does that matter to you?"—is the kindest question you can ask. It means I am interested in you as a human being. This is how advice or help gets replaced with curiosity.

> One of the basic elements of the relationship between oppressor and oppressed is prescription. Every prescription represents the imposition of one individual's choice upon another, transforming the consciousness of the person prescribed to into one that conforms with the prescriber's consciousness.
>
> Paolo Freire, *The Pedagogy of the Oppressed*

The future hinges on this issue. Advice, recommendations, and obvious actions are exactly what increase the likelihood that tomorrow will be just like yesterday.

Ask Lower-Risk Questions First

Certain questions require a greater level of trust among citizens than others. A good design begins with less demanding questions and ends with the more difficult ones. The conversations of ownership, commitment, and gifts are high risk and require greater trust to have meaning. Discussions of crossroads, possibility, and dissent are easier and come earlier—this will become clearer in the coming chapters.

Example: Possibility over Problem Solving

As a foundation executive in Columbus, Ohio, Phil Cass was part of a group bringing many of the ideas in this book into the health care debate. Using a methodology developed in Europe called the Art of Hosting, the group created a series of community conversations involving a cross section of several hundred citizens in reimagining and ultimately reforming health care. Their understanding of the importance of the question and how the conversation is framed produced gatherings with profound results: the conversation has shifted from how to reform the existing health care system to how to create a system that nurtures the health and well-being of each citizen of that community. The cynic would say that this is just semantics; the activist who believes the future is waiting to be created would know that the transformation has begun.

Six Conversations

Before I make these ideas more concrete, here is a quick overview of the larger story we are creating:

Powerful questions give us the means to initiate a community where accountability and commitment are ingrained. They are a key to understanding the means and architecture for gathering people in a way that will build relatedness, which in turn creates communities in which citizens will choose accountability and commitment. This is what overcomes our fragmentation and reduces our tendency to demand change from people who are essentially strangers to us.

The thinking follows this logic: the strategy for an alternative future is to focus on ways to shift context, build relatedness, and create space for a more intentional possibility.

This strategy gives form to the idea that if you can change context and relatedness in this room, you have changed the context and relatedness in the world, at least for this moment.

The way we change the room is by changing the conversation. Not to just any new conversation, but to one that creates communal accountability and commitment. This new conversation is almost always initiated in the form of a question.

We are avoiding conversations that are just talk. Certain conversations are satisfying and true, yet they have no power and entail no accountability.

For example:

> Telling the history of how we got here
>
> Giving explanations and opinions
>
> Blaming and complaining
>
> Making reports and descriptions
>
> Carefully defining terms and conditions
>
> Retelling your story again and again
>
> Seeking quick action

These are the conventional conversations and are often conducted through conferences, press releases, trainings, master plans, and the call for more studies and expertise. They are well intentioned and have face validity, but don't change anything. Most of what we want to see changed has been explained, complained about, reported on, and defined for decades.

"Just-talk" conversations can help us get connected or increase our understanding of who we are, but we endure them mostly out of habit, for they are so ingrained in the social convention of our culture that if we didn't have them, we would miss them. They do not, however, contribute to transformation. Here are the conversations that produce something more than just talk:

> Invitation
>
> Possibility
>
> Ownership
>
> Dissent
>
> Commitment
>
> Gifts

Each of these conversations leads to the others. Any one held wholeheartedly takes us to and resolves all the others. When any of them are absent, it is just talk, no matter how urgent the cause, how important the plan, how elegant the answer.

CHAPTER 11

Invitation

The first of the six conversations that create an accountable and hospitable community is invitation. Once the invitation
conversation takes place, we follow with the conversations of possibility,
ownership, dissent, commitment, and gifts.

*Invitation is the means through which hospitality is created. Invita-
tion counters the conventional belief that change requires mandate or
persuasion. Invitation honors the importance of choice, the necessary
condition for accountability. We begin with the question "Whom do we
want in the room?" For starters, we want people who are not used to
being together. Then we include the six elements of a powerful invitation: naming the possibility about which we are convening, being clear
about whom we invite, emphasizing freedom of choice in showing up,
specifying what is required of each should they choose to attend, making a clear request, and making the invitation as personal as possible.*

• • •

As we enter the conversations for structuring belonging,
a caveat: real life is circuitous; it does not develop the way the
conversations appear on a page. Except for the invitation, deciding which
conversations to have, in which order, will vary with the context of a gathering. Since all the conversations lead to each other, sequence is not critical.
The conversations described here and in the next chapter, though, appear
in the rough order that usually aligns with the logic of people's experience.

Conversation One: The Invitation

Hospitality, the welcoming of strangers, is the essence of a restorative community. Historically, if strangers knocked at your door, you automatically invited them in. They would be fed and offered a place to sleep, even if they were your enemies. As long as they were in your house, they were safe from harm. They were treated as if they belonged, regardless of the past. This is the context of restoration we are seeking. Our hospitality begins with an invitation. The invitation is to those who have an interest in the future you are imagining—*all* who have that interest, whether like-minded people, strangers, stakeholders, adversaries, or someone who is not known, yet. Whom you invite into the room is a big choice.

The conversation for invitation is the decision to engage other citizens to be part of the possibility that we are committed to. The invitation is in itself an act of generosity, and the mere act of inviting may have more meaning than anything that happens in the gathering. Even for those who do not show up.

An invitation is more than just a request to attend; it is a call to create an alternative future, to join in the possibility we have declared. The question is, "What is the invitation we can make for people to participate in creating a community of connectedness and purpose, regardless of their story or past actions?"

The Distinction for the Invitation Conversation

The distinction here is between invitation and the more typical ways of achieving change: mandate and persuasive marketing. The belief in mandate and persuasion triggers talk about how to change other people, how to get those people on board, how to make showing up a requirement, all of which are simply questions driven by our desire to control others. What is distinct about an invitation is that it can be refused, at no cost to the one refusing.

An authentic invitation operates without promising incentives or rewards. Offering inducements such as door prizes, gifts, or a celebrity attraction diminishes the clarity of choice of those invited. The lack of induce-ment keeps a level playing field. When we try to induce people to show up through strong selling or the language of enrolling, we are adding subtle pressure that, in a small but important way, blurs the freely taken decision to say yes.

David Bornstein's research describes how real transformation occurs only through choice. It cannot be sold or mandated. This is particularly true with transformation in community. Institutions and systems can mandate change or attendance from employees because they are under a legal con-tract. If you don't show up, you violate the contract. This leads to a discussion of consequences, which are very popular in a patriarchal control world.

In an authentic community, citizens decide anew every single time whether to show up. Of course it makes a difference if people do not show up, but we keep inviting them again and again. If they do not choose to show up, there are *no* consequences. They are always welcome. As it is with friends and family. This is what makes volunteer work so maddening—you never know who will show up. The freedom of choice without consequences is also its source of power, for when people do freely decide to show up, it means something more.

The Risks of Invitation

The anxiety of invitation is that if we give people a choice, they might not show up. I do not want to face the reality of their absence, caution, reserva-tions, passivity, or indifference. I do not want to have to face the prospect that I or a few of us may be alone in the future we want to pursue.

And I do not want to face the same truth about myself, for my fear that they will not come is the caution I feel myself about showing up, even for the possibility that I am committed to. My fear is that what I long for is not possible, that what I invite them to is not realistic, that the world I seek cannot exist. And so I imagine myself as a misplaced person, an exile. It is today's version of an old story that I am wrong and will soon be found out. The fear that no one will show up is a projection of my own doubt, my loss of faith.

Even when we have the power to mandate attendance, the risk is that when I instruct them to show up, they will come and what I will get is lip service. They may not support the intentions or vision that gave rise to the invitation. The patriarchal fear is that without restraints, incentives, and the use of acceptable force, nothing will get done. The argument for patriarchy is that there are tasks in which choice—another term for engaging the whole person—is not required or will not contribute to accomplishing the task. This may be true, but the limitation of this stance is that even though tomorrow may be a little better, the future will be very much like the past.

The Radical Aspect of Invitation

If the essence of community is to create structures for belonging, then we are constantly inviting people who are strangers to us, and one another, into the circle. An invitation is the antidote to our projection onto those we think are the problem. We take back our projection by extending ourselves to strangers. We make the invitation, in the face of our own isolation, of having been waiting to be invited, of wanting others to take the first step, of wanting others to reach out to us, acknowledge us, and give us the gold star that never came at the right moment. This will never happen, so we are obligated to take the first step.

Invitation may seem simple and straightforward, but it is not. Especially for introverts like me. I have never attended a party without wondering if I had the right night, and have never given a party without believing no one would come.

Example: Ken Murphy: A Seminar with Purpose and Nothing Practical

My friend and client Ken Murphy and I wanted to convene a Humanities Series for people working in human resources (HR) at Philip Morris, where Ken worked at the time. The intent of the series was unusual. It was to imagine a new possibility for HR and to do it by bringing faculty in from outside the field. We selected our faculty: a poet, a philosopher, a theater director, an improvisation actor, a nun, and a city manager. Not your typical faculty for a workshop inside a traditional, high-control system.

Our belief was that these people would open our thinking and create space for something new. We also agreed that the series was not designed for better performance, for greater efficiency, or to provide new skills. The invitation would declare that we were interested only in new thinking and that we were therefore offering nothing practical, nothing that could be applied to the job in the short run. We also planned to state that the relevance of the experience would be in the hands of the participants. We would make no request of the faculty to ensure the relevance of their presentation.

It took us two years to get up the nerve to make this invitation. All these people worked for Ken, so if he had just called a typical meeting or training session, they all would have come. What was interesting was that as straightforward as the invitation might seem (they either come or they don't), giving people real choice in the midst of a patriarchal business institution felt like a radical act. For any of us to offer others real choice in something we care about is always a risk.

Genuine invitation changes our relationship with others, for we come to them as an equal. I must be willing to take no for an answer, without resorting to various forms of persuasion. To sell or induce is not operating by invitation. It is using the language of invitation as a subtle form of control.

This rather purist version of invitation offers one reason why you cannot judge success by numbers of people or scale. The pressure for scale will distort the integrity of the invitation. What caused Ken and me to finally go ahead with our Humanities Series was deciding that if only five people accepted the invitation, that would be a beginning and worth the effort. As it turned out, we had fifty seats open, and they were taken immediately. And after every session, the feedback was consistent: thank you for giving me the space to think on my own, share with others, and not have to worry about pleasing the faculty by reassuring them that what they offered was useful and immediately applicable. This is a glimpse into the face of freedom.

Invitation as a Way of Being

Invitation is not only a step in bringing people together but also a fundamental way of being in community. It manifests the willingness to live in a collaborative way. This means that a future can be created without having to force it or sell it or barter for it. When we believe that barter or subtle coercion is necessary, we are operating out of a context of scarcity and self-interest, the core currencies of the economist. Barter or coercion seems necessary when we have little faith in citizens' desire and capacity to operate out of idealism. The choice for idealism or cynicism is a spiritual stance about the nature of human beings. Cynicism gets justified by naming itself "reality."

A commitment to invitation is a core strategy for idealism and determines the context within which people show up. For all the agony of a volunteer effort, you are rewarded by being in the room with people who are up to something larger than their immediate self-interest. People who want to be there, even if their numbers are few. The concern we have about the turnout is simply an expression of our own doubts about the possibility that given a free choice, people will choose to create a future distinct from the past.

Invitation is a language act. "I invite you." Period. This is a powerful conversation because at the moment of inviting, hospitality and choice are created in the world.

• • •

There are certain properties of invitation that can make it more than simply a request. In addition to stating the reason for the gathering, an invitation at its best must contain a hurdle or demand if accepted. This is not to be inhospitable but to make even the act of invitation an example of the interdependence we want to experience.

So the invitation is a request not only to show up but to engage. It declares, "We want you to come, but if you do, something will be required from you." Too many leadership initiatives or programs are begun with a sales and marketing mind-set: How do we seduce people to sign up and feel good about doing things they may not want to do? Real change is a self-inflicted wound. People need to self-enroll in order to experience their freedom and commitment. Let this begin in the decision to attend, knowing there is a price to be paid far beyond the cost of time and perhaps money.

The Invitation List

The first critical question to ask about what is needed for something different to occur in the world is Kathie Dannemiller's classic: "Who do we need in the room?"

The intent is to bring together people across boundaries. Each person who convenes has a network of relationships with people who might have a stake or interest in the possibility. The challenge is to include the "other" in the conversation. We have to let go of our story about the past. This means we keep inviting those who have not been in the conversation. Even if people say no, that act itself is important and counts for something.

This means that we constantly seek to have people in the room who are not used to being together. In most cases this would bring together people across sectors (business, education, social services, activists) and, more important (though rare), across economic and social classes. Hard work to make this happen, but perhaps more important than what occurs in the gathering.

Marvin Weisbord and Sandra Janoff have given a nice structure to this question in their book *Don't Just Do Something, Stand There!* They want a sample of the "whole system" in the room when they convene for change. They want people with

Authority to act—decision makers;

Resources, such as contacts, time, or money;

Expertise in the issues to be considered;

Information about the topic that no others have;

A need to be involved because they will be affected by the outcome and can speak to the consequences.

The decision about whom to invite is an act of leadership that in and of itself carries a message. Many we invite will choose not to come. This recognizes that for every gathering, there are going to be people who would be useful, but are not in the room. This is forever the case. It still means that whoever shows up are the right people. Eventually those who do show up always have the task of deciding whom to invite next.

Constructing the Invitation

The elements of invitation are the following:

- Declare the possibility of the gathering
- Frame the choice
- Name the hurdle
- Reinforce the request
- Decide on the most personal form possible

Declare the Possibility

The invitation is activated by the possibility we are committed to. This becomes the reason for the gathering. The possibility is a declaration of the future that the convener is committed to. We need to work hard on a statement of possibility that is compelling to others and also inspires us.

Example: The Possibility of a Safe Cincinnati

Harriet Kaufman is committed to the possibility of a safe and peaceful Cincinnati. She believes that what is needed is a conversation that treats violence as a public health issue. She has issued a series of invitations for people to participate in a community conversation and requires that they engage as active citizens and not come to listen to some experts talk. The moment she makes her invitation, she has brought her possibility into the community.

For Harriet Kaufman's possibility of a safe and peaceful community, she keeps inviting all who have a stake in peace. Youth, public safety, faith community, parents, activists, local government, and more are invited—every time. Everyone in her network gets invited every time. Some show up, some don't; some like the conversation, some don't. Some think violence is a problem for the experts to solve, or a youth problem, or a police problem. Harriet sees the violence and thinks of the possibility of safety and peace. When Harriet enters the room, safety and peace come with her.

You might ask at this point, what results did she get? What was accomplished? How many people showed up? Irrelevant questions. Harriet was and is an ambassador for peace. That counts.

Frame the Choice

We need to pay attention to our willingness and comfort in accepting refusal. This is a whole other conversation discussed later, but for now I'll just say that for an invitation to be authentic, refusal has to be perfectly acceptable. The invitation must allow room for a no. If no is not an option, then it is not an invitation. Framing the choice means we need to be clear that we will not initiate consequences for not attending and that we respect someone's decision not to attend. We choose to have faith that there are good reasons for others not attending what is important to us. Let them know that even if they say no now, they will always be welcome in the future.

Name the Hurdle

We need to tell people explicitly what is required of them should they choose to attend. There is a price to pay for their decision to attend. They will be asked to explore ways to deepen their learning and commitment. Here are some other common hurdles that should be part of the invitation: plan to engage with "others," put your interests aside for the moment, commit to the time, and be willing to postpone quick action.

For one series of conversations across boundaries that we held in one section of Cincinnati, we asked people to postpone problem solving and the negotiation of interests. They were not asked to compromise their interests or their constituents' interests but just to hold them to the side for the time being. Here is what the invitation looked like:

1. We come together to create a new possibility for Over the Rhine, an urban neighborhood. We promise to have a conversation we have not had before. We do not come together to negotiate interests, share our stories, or problem-solve the past or future.

2. No one will be asked in any way to yield on their commitments or interests. We are not coming to decide anything. We begin with the belief that the commitments and interests of each of us have to be honored and taken into account by all.

3. Each agrees to participate in all three two-hour discussions. There are always emergencies, and always pressing priorities, but the loss of even one person, for just one meeting, immensely reduces our chance of success.

The most important point is that they were told they would be asked to talk at length, and hopefully strengthen their relationships, with people they have a "story" about. The result was a durable effort to create an African American Quarter in this area. It was never really accomplished. The effort, though, brought people together, which had ripple effects beyond what we had imagined.

Paradoxically, even though there is no cost for refusing the invitation, there is a price for coming. Everything that has value has a price. Make the purchase price explicit, so that the act of showing up carries some accountability.

Naming the hurdle in the invitation gives us traction in the meeting. When people start to complain, sit in the back of the room, act as if they do not want to be here, and do all the small but noticeable things that hold back the action, we can stand on the fact that they knew what the deal was and still showed up. This gives us the right to ask them what they are doing here. It gives us traction in moving people past their typical story. When they give their habitual explanation about who else needs to change, we can deal with this in a new way, simply because the agreement was clear as to what would be required of them.

The best invitation I have run across, which got a lot of attention for a while, was from Ernest Shackleton, who in the early 1900s was recruiting for an Antarctic expedition. Supposedly he ran an ad in the London *Times* that read: "Wanted: Men for Antarctic Expedition. Low Pay. Lousy Food. Safe Return Doubtful." Perfect. He reportedly got five thousand applicants.

Reinforce the Request

End the invitation by telling people that you want them to come and that if they choose not to attend, they will be missed but not forgotten.

Make It Personal

In an electronic, need-for-speed, texting, and email world, the more personal the invitation the better. A visit is more personal than a call; a call is more personal than a letter; a letter is more personal than email. A letter with six people's names on it is less personal than one addressed to one person, and an email is about as impersonal as it gets. We are so flooded with emails and the medium is so senseless that I have come to believe that in the rank order of inviting, emails don't count. But all are better than lying in bed at night waiting for the universe to provide.

CHAPTER 12

The Possibility, Ownership, Dissent, Commitment, and Gifts Conversations

Following the invitation, there are five other conversations for structuring belonging: possibility, ownership, dissent, commitment, and gifts. Since all the conversations lead to each other, sequence is not that critical. The context of the gathering will often determine which questions to deal with and at what depth. It's important to understand, though, that some conversations are more difficult than others, especially in communities where citizens are just beginning to engage with one another. I present them in ascending order of difficulty, with possibility generally an early conversation to have and gifts typically one of the more difficult.

We are using possibility here in a unique way. Possibility is not a goal or prediction; it is the statement of a future condition that is beyond reach. It works on us and evolves from a discussion of personal crossroads. It is an act of imagination of what we can create together, and it takes the form of a declaration, best made publicly.

The ownership conversation asks citizens to act as if they were creating what exists in the world. Confession is the religious and judicial version of ownership. The distinction is between ownership and blame. The questions for ownership are "How valuable do you plan for this gathering to be?" "How have we each contributed to the current situation?" and "What is the story you hold about this community and your place in it?" It is important for people to see the limitation of their story, for each story has a payoff and a cost. Naming these is a precondition to creating an alternative future.

The dissent conversation creates an opening for commitment. The questions explicitly ask for doubts and reservations. The distinction is between dissent and complaint. When the dissents are expressed, we need to just listen. Don't solve them, defend against them, or explain anything. People's doubts, cynicism, and resignation are theirs alone. Not to be taken on by us. Dissent is distinct from denial, rebellion, and resignation. The questions for dissent are about doubts, refusal, retracting commitments we no longer want to fulfill, owning our lack of forgiveness, and naming our unexpressed resentments.

The commitment conversation is a promise with no expectation of return. Virtue is its own reward. Commitment is distinguished from barter. The enemy of commitment is not opposition but lip service. The commitments that count the most are ones made to peers, other citizens. Not ones made to or by leaders. The questions are variations of "What is the promise I am willing to make?" We have to create space for citizens to declare that there is no promise they are willing to make at this time. Refusal to promise does not cost us our membership or seat at the table. We only lose our seat when we do not honor our word.

The most radical and uncomfortable conversation is about our gifts. The leadership and citizen task is to bring the gifts of those on the margin into the center. The gifts conversation is the essence of valuing diversity and inclusion. We are not defined by deficiencies or what is missing. We are defined by our gifts and what is present. This is so for individuals and for communities. Belonging occurs when we tell others what gift we receive from them, especially in this moment. When this occurs, in the presence of others, community is built. We embrace our own destiny when we have the courage to acknowledge our own gifts and choose to bring them into the world. The questions for the gift conversations are "What is the gift you still hold in exile?" "What is it about you that no one knows?" "What gratitude has gone unexpressed?" and "What have others in this room done that has touched you?"

• • •

Conversation Two: Possibility

The possibility conversation frees us to be pulled by a new future. The distinction is between a possibility, which lives into the future, and problem solving, which makes improvements on the past. This distinction takes its value from an understanding that living systems are propelled by the force of the future, and *possibility* as we use it here (thank you, Werner) is one way of speaking of the future.

Possibility occurs as a declaration, and wholeheartedly declaring a possibility can, in fact, be the transformation. The leadership task is to postpone problem solving and stay focused on possibility until it is spoken with resonance and passion. The good news is that once we have fully declared a possibility, it works on us—we do not have to work on it.

The Distinctions for the Possibility Conversation

The challenge with possibility is that it gets confused with vision, goals, prediction, and optimism. Possibility is not about what we plan to have happen or what we think will happen or whether things will get better. Goals, prediction, and optimism don't create anything; they just might make things a little better and cheer us up in the process. Nor is possibility simply a dream. Dreaming leaves us bystanders or observers of our lives. Possibility creates something new. It is a declaration of a future that has the quality of being and aliveness that we choose to live into. It is framed as a declaration of the world that I want to inhabit. It is a statement of who I am that transcends our history, our story, our usual demographics. The power is in the act of declaring.

The distinction between possibility and problem solving is worth dwelling on for a moment. As I have said, surely too many times, we traditionally start with problem solving and talk about goals, targets, resources, and how to persuade others. Even the creation of a vision is part of the problem-solving mentality. A vision is something we must wait for to realize and is most often followed by an effort to make it concrete and practical. Even a vision, which is a more imaginative form of problem solving, needs to be postponed and replaced with possibility. The future is created through a declaration of what the possibility is that we stand for. Out of this declaration, each time we enter a room, the possibility enters with us.

The communal possibility comes into being through individual public declarations of possibility. Much the same as witnessing in religious gatherings. Though every possibility begins as an individual declaration, it gains power and impacts community when made public. The community possibility is not the aggregation of individual possibilities. Nor is it a negotiation or agreement on common possibility. The communal possibility is that space or porous container where a collective exists for the realization of all the possibilities of its members. This is the real meaning of a restorative community. It is that place where all possibilities can come alive, and they come alive at the moment they are announced.

●　●　●

The possibility conversation gives form to one way the gifts of those in the margin get brought into the center. Each person's possibility counts, especially those of people whose voices are quieted or marginalized by the drumbeat of retribution. In fact, what distinguishes those on the margin in communities is that they tragically live without real possibility. For many youth on the margin, the future is narrow, perhaps death or prison. They have trouble imagining a future distinct from the past or present. This is the real tragedy: not only that life is difficult but that it is a life that holds no possibility for a different future.

Just to be clear about the whole process: The possibility conversation alone does not restore community. The other conversations are just as critical. We have to act as owners of our community, there has to be space for dissent, a commitment has to be made, and gifts have to be embraced. Each conversation takes its life and impact from the other conversations. Even though each leads to the others, any one of them held in isolation reduces the chance of real transformation.

The Questions for the Possibility Conversation

There needs to be a point during each gathering when time is devoted to the private possibility to be developed and then made public. This works best in two separate steps. The best opening question for possibility is

What is the crossroads where you find yourself at this stage of your life or work or in the project around which we are assembled?

Later, the more direct individual question for possibility will be

What declaration of possibility can you make that has the power to transform the community and inspire you?

There are two overarching questions that point to the future but cannot be asked directly:

What do we want to create together that would make the difference?

What can we create together that we cannot create alone?

These two questions almost define community, for community is that place where these questions are valued. The challenge is that I have never seen them answered in a meaningful way when asked within a context of isolation and disengagement. When people who do not really know each other gather, they are incapable of answering the questions in this most direct and purposeful form. That is why we need the other conversations.

Conversation Three: Ownership

Accountability is the willingness to acknowledge that we have participated in creating, through commission or omission, the conditions that we wish to see changed. If we lack this capacity to see ourselves as cause, our efforts become either coercive or wishfully dependent on the transformation of others.

Community will be created the moment we decide to act as creators of what it can become. This is the stance of ownership, which is available to us every moment on every issue, even world peace, the overdependence on fossil fuel consumption, and the fact that our teenagers are slightly self-centered.

This requires us to believe that this organization, this neighborhood, this community is mine or ours to create. This will occur when we are willing to answer the essential question, "How have I contributed to creating the current reality?" Confusion, blame, and waiting for someone else to change are defenses against ownership and personal power. This core question, when answered, is central to how the community is transformed.

Innocence and indifference are subtle denials of ownership. The future is denied with the response, "It doesn't matter to me—whatever you want to do is fine." This is always a lie and just a polite way of avoiding a difficult conversation around ownership.

People best create that which they own, and cocreation is the bedrock of accountability. The ownership conversation most directly deals with the belief that each of us, perhaps even from the moment of birth, is cause, not effect. Again, the leadership task is to find a way to use this conversation to confront people with their freedom.

The Distinctions for the Conversation for Ownership

Ownership is the decision to acknowledge our guilt. To confess that the world is, in part, our construction. In this way, we become the author of our own experience. It is the choice to decide on our own what value and meaning will occur when we show up. It is the stance that each of us is creating the world, even the one we have inherited.

The key distinction for the conversation is between ownership and blame (a form of entitlement).

We have to realize that each time people enter a room, they walk in with ambivalence, wondering whether this is the right place to be. This is because their default mind-set is that someone else owns the room, the meeting, and the purpose that convened the meeting.

Every conventional gathering begins with the unspoken belief that whoever called the meeting has something in mind for us. We are inundated with the world trying to sell us something, so much so that we cannot imagine that this time will be different. This is why so much talk is about others not in the room.

The leader/convener has to act to change this, in a sense to renegotiate the social contract. We want to shift to the belief that this world, including this gathering, is ours to construct together. The intent is to move the social contract from parenting to partnership. Renegotiating the social contract for this room is a metaphorical example of how our social contract with the community can also be renegotiated.

The Questions for Ownership

Questions that address the idea that "I am cause" can be difficult to take on immediately, so lower-risk questions precede a direct approach on this one. The best opening questions are those about the ownership that people feel for this particular gathering. The extent to which they act as owners of this meeting is symptomatic of how they will act as owners of the larger question on the table. The extent of our ownership for larger questions is more difficult and therefore requires a higher level of relatedness before it can be held in the right context.

Here is a series of questions that have the capacity to shift the ownership of the room.

Four Early Questions

The most effective way to renegotiate the social contract is to ask people to rate on a 7-point scale, from low to high, their responses to four questions:

How valuable an experience (or project or community) do you plan for this to be?

How much risk are you willing to take?

How participative do you plan to be?

To what extent are you invested in the well-being of the whole?

These are the four questions to ask early in any gathering. People answer them individually, then share their answers in a small group. As mentioned earlier, be sure to remind them not to give advice, be helpful, or cheer anyone up. Just get interested in whatever the answers are.

The Guilt Question

At some later point, we need to ask the essential question on which account-ability hinges:

What have I done to contribute to the very thing I complain about or want to change?

Sometimes people will talk about how hard they have tried to make things better. Nice answer, but not to this question. This question, higher risk than most others, is about what you have done to interfere with the community's well-being. For people to answer it requires a great deal of trust. It can be asked only after people are connected to each other. This may be the most transforming question of all. If I do not see my part in causing the past and the present, then there is no possible way I can participate usefully in being a coauthor of the future.

The Story Questions

Another ownership conversation is to confront our stories, the stories we talked of earlier that limit the possibility of an alternative future. Werner Erhard is so brilliantly clear and creative about this issue. The sequence he has put together, which I have adapted, goes like this:

What is the story about this community or organization that you hear yourself most often telling? The one that you are wedded to and maybe even take your identity from?

Then ask:

What are the payoffs you receive from holding on to this story?

The payoffs are usually in the neighborhood of being right, being in control, being safe. Or not being wrong, controlled, or at risk.
And finally:

What is your attachment to this story costing you?

The cost, most often, is our sense of aliveness. Perhaps our faith.
These are the questions that allow us to complete our stories. Not forget them, but complete them. The naming of the story to another, in the context

we have created, can take the limiting power out of the story. This allows the story to stay in the past and creates an opening for us to move forward.

A friendly warning: don't ever underestimate the determination of people to hold on to their stories, no matter the cost or the suffering they sustain. Most of us are not willing to give up our story in the moment, but this process works on us over time.

Conversation Four: Dissent

Creating space for dissent is the way diversity gets valued in the world. Inviting dissent into the conversation is how we show respect for a wide range of beliefs. It honors Bohr's maxim that for every great idea, the opposite idea is also true.

There is no way to be awake and to care about a purpose or a place or a project without having serious doubts and reservations. Each of us takes many walks in the desert, and in some ways our faith is measured by the extent of our doubts. Without doubt, our faith has no meaning, no substance; it is purchased at too small a price to give it value.

This sounds simple and true enough, but in a patriarchal world, dissent is considered disloyalty. Or negativism. Or not being a team player. Or not being a good citizen. America, love it or leave it. You are either with us or against us. This is a corruption of hospitality and friendship. Hospitality is the welcoming not only of strangers but also of the strange ideas and beliefs they bring with them.

Doubt and Dissent

A critical task of leadership is to protect space for the expression of people's doubts. The act of surfacing doubts and dissent does not deflect the communal intention to create something new. What is critical, and hard to live with, is that leaders do not have to respond to each person's doubts. None of us do. Authentic dissent is complete simply in its expression. When we think we have to answer people's doubts and defend ourselves, then the space for dissent closes down. When people have doubts and we attempt to answer them, we are colluding with their reluctance to be accountable for their own future. All we have to do with the doubts of others is get interested in them. We do not have to take them on or let them resonate with our own doubts. We just get interested.

Example: Police and Citizens

One place where doubt and dissent are least understood is in the relationship between police and citizens. Few civil servants put themselves at such risk or are more vulnerable than the police. No civil servants are literally more physically present in a community than police. They walk or ride our streets, show up when we go out of control. They come to our homes when families are caving in. They also are constantly in community conversations about public safety. These safety conversations can be intense, and this is often because citizens project their anxiety onto the police, and the police absorb the projection and feel that they are on trial and need to defend themselves. This does not have to be true, if we can value dissent as healing in its own way. Not easy.

At the core, police get into a problem when they think they are *responsible* for public safety—and when this belief is matched by citizens. The police are not responsible for my safety. Citizens who believe that the police are responsible for safety are avoiding their own accountability. Citizens are responsible for public safety; citizens commit crimes, prevent crimes, and create the conditions where crime is high or low. As long as police take responsibility for safety, they are going to stay in a defensive stance, which moves nothing forward. Police are responsible for enforcing the law, apprehending criminals, and mediating or stopping violence. Police are not suppliers of safety to a passive citizenry. Safety is not a product purchased from the police. When citizens want to place responsibility for safety on the police, and police defend themselves, they collude with citizens' unwillingness to claim their sidewalks and community as their own.

Listening is the action step for the police that replaces defending themselves. Listening, understanding at a deeper level than is being expressed, is the action that creates a restorative community. This does not mean that police, in this case, do not need to change or be involved in later problem solving; of course they do, as do the rest of us. It does mean that instead of answering every question, defending their actions, they can ask questions to find out more about the concerns, the doubts, and even the lives of citizens. No one understands this more than Mike Butler, police chief of Longmont, Colorado. One of Mike's favorite statements is: "For 80 percent of the calls we receive, people do not need a uniformed officer; they need a neighbor." Wise man.

This then is a key role of leadership: get interested in people's dissent, their doubts, and find out why this matters so much to them. Dissent becomes commitment and accountability when we get interested in it without having to fix, explain, or answer it. Granted, sometimes other things masquerade as authentic dissent, which will be discussed a little later.

"No" Is the Beginning of Commitment

The dissent conversation begins by allowing people the space to say no. It rests on the belief that if we cannot say no, then our yes has no meaning.

Each of us needs the chance to express our doubts and reservations, without having to justify them or to move quickly into problem solving. "No" is the beginning of the conversation for commitment. This is critical: dissent is followed by the other conversations. To hold dissent productively is not to leave it hanging there but to see it as a transitional conversation taking us to the other conversations of possibility, ownership, and gifts.

The fear is that we will make people more negative by giving them room for refusal. The mental model of the ostrich. If people say no, it does not create their dissent; it only expresses it. It also does not mean they will get their way. Restorative community is that place where saying no doesn't cost us our membership in the meeting or in the community. Encourage those who say no to stay—we need their voice.

We will let go of only those doubts that we have given voice to. When someone authentically says no, then the room becomes real and trustworthy. An authentic statement is one in which the person owns that the dissent is their choice and not a form of blame or complaint. The power in the expression of doubts is that it gives us choice about the doubts. Once expressed, they no longer control us; we control them.

Doubt and "no" are symbolic expressions of people finding their space and role in the future. It is when we fully understand what people do not want that choice becomes possible. Dissent in this way is life giving, or life affirming. It is the refusal to live the life someone else has in mind for us. For individuals, it is the moment when we acknowledge that we are not the children our parents, guardians, teachers had in mind for us. We have disappointed others and for too long internalized that disappointment. The moment we say no to the expectations of others about who they wish us to be, the moment we declare, "I am not that person; I am not the son or daughter you had in mind," our adulthood begins. Just because it took thirty or forty years, this is no time to get picky.

Same in community. The moment people experience their capacity to dissent or, in softer form, express doubts, and not lose their place in the circle, they begin to join as full-fledged citizens. When dissent is truly valued and becomes the object of genuine curiosity, the chances of showing up as an owner of that circle, that room, that neighborhood go up dramatically. When the police understand this, the relationship changes. The police can then join with citizens in the discussion of how citizens can produce their own safety. This is what works, especially in the most difficult neighborhoods.

The Distinctions for the Conversation for Dissent

There is a vital difference between authentic dissent and inauthentic dissent, which we can call false refusal. Inauthentic forms of dissent are denial, rebellion, and resignation.

Denial means we act as if the present is good enough. It is defense against the woundedness of the present and a rejection of any possibility beyond continuous improvement. Our denial of the destruction of the environment is a good example. Denial in this case takes the form of wanting more data or holding the belief that technology is a god that can surmount any obstacle. Denial often agrees there is a problem, but then trivializes its existence or its cost. Climate denial is really about cost and inconvenience, always the argument against the common good.

Denial is a defining feature of addiction. In creating the communities we live in, we are addicted to urban centers and rural towns that don't work for all, to a world of large class differences, to a place where we consider people on the margin not to be our brothers and sisters. We are addicted to accepting the illusion of safety that we get from allowing large systems to control the solutions for our communities. They control the development conversation; they promote their solutions to poverty that require more schooling and more training, and treat people in exile as if it was their fault. Hard to accept that you are a player in creating what you are trying so hard to eliminate.

Rebellion is more complex. It lives in reaction to the world. On the surface, rebellion claims to be against monarchy, dominion, or oppression. Too often it turns out to be a vote *for* monarchy, dominion, or patriarchy. Rebellion is most often not a call for transformation or a new context but simply a complaint that others control the monarchy and not us. This is why most revolutions fail—because nothing changes, only the name of the monarch.

The community form of rebellion is protest. It is noble in tradition, but still often keeps us in perpetual reaction to the stances of others. There is safety in building an identity on what we do not want. The extremists on both sides of any issue are more wedded to their positions than to creating a new possibility. That is why they make unfulfillable demands. The AM radio band is populated with this nonconversation. So is the blog world. Any time we act in reaction, even to evil, we are giving power to what we are reacting to.

I have heard John McKnight say that advisory groups speak quietly to power, protestors scream at power, and neither chooses to reclaim or produce power. The real problem with rebellion is that it is such fun. It avoids taking responsibility, operates on the high ground, is fueled by righteousness, gives legitimacy to blame, and is a delightful escape from the unbearable burden of being accountable. It brings great value when it occurs; it teaches us, holds us accountable. Occupy Wall Street was a useful wake-up call, but it was too easy to fall asleep after its moment. There was little in its framing of the issue that held citizens accountable for what they do with their money or how they think about their own choice to depart from the free-market culture.

Resignation is the ultimate act of powerlessness and a stance against possibility. It is a passive form of control. It is born of our cynicism and loss of faith. What we are resigning from is the future, and what we are embracing is the past. None of us is strong enough to carry the dead weight of others' resignation or even our own. Resignation ultimately alienates us and destroys community. It is the spiritual cause of isolation and not belonging. Beware of resignation, for it presents itself as if data and experience were on its side.

Here, then, is the point: Dissent, as a form of refusal, becomes authentic when it is a choice for its own sake. When it is an act of accountability. Authentic dissent is recognizable by the absence of blame, the absence of resignation. Blame, denial, rebellion, and resignation have no power to create. A simple *no* begins a larger conversation, or at least creates the space for one.

This is most clearly embodied when we realize there is nothing to argue about. Once again, when faced with a no, or doubts, or authentic refusal, we move forward when we get interested and curious. The ultimate expression of useful power is a leader's saying, "I must warn you that if you argue with me, I will likely be forced to take your side."

The Questions for Dissent

The challenge, then, is to frame the questions in a way that evokes dissent that is authentic. We do not want to encourage, through our selection of questions, any kind of denial, rebellion, or resignation. To circumvent denial, don't ask people whether they think there is a problem. Or even ask them to define the problem. Do not ask people what they are going to do, or to list the ten characteristics of anything. The way to avoid rebellion is to stop trying to sell or control the world. When faced with rebellion, all we can do is recognize it, not argue.

Some questions for the expression of dissent:

What doubts and reservations do you have?

What is the no, or refusal, that you keep postponing?

What have you said yes to that you no longer really mean?

What is a commitment or decision that you have changed your mind about?

What forgiveness are you withholding?

What resentment do you hold that no one knows about?

These are in ascending order of difficulty. The final two are very diffi-cult and should be used with discretion. I always offer them as a possible conversation, for I know that if people do not want to answer a question, they won't, and no damage is done. We can ask anything, as long as we do not pressure people in any way to answer.

The key for the leader/convener is not to take the dissent personally or to argue in any way with the doubts that get expressed. If you can genuinely answer a question that resolves the doubt, then do so. Most of the time, however, the doubts are well founded and have no easy answer, so all we can do is appreciate that the doubt was made public.

The intent is for concerns to be expressed openly, not left to quiet con-versations in the hallways, among allies, or in the restrooms. Dissent is a form of caring, not of resistance.

Conversation Five: Commitment

Commitment usually comes later in the process, after the first four conver-sations and some of the work on substantive issues has been done.

Commitment is a promise made with no expectation of return. It is the willingness to make a promise independent of either approval or reciprocity from other people. This takes barter out of the conversation. Our promise is not contingent on the actions of others. The economist is replaced by the artist. As long as our promise is dependent on the actions of others, it is not a commitment; it is a deal, a contract. A bargained future is not an alternative future; it is more of the past brought forward.

The declaration of a promise is the form that commitment takes; that is the action that initiates change. It is one thing to set a goal or objective, but something more personal to use the language of promises. Plus, to the extent that a promise is a sacred form of expression, this language anoints the space in the asking.

Lip Service Is the Enemy of Commitment

Sometimes we act as if we need to choose between commitment and refusal or dissent. They are friendly to each other, and both are important conversations. Saying no is a stance as useful as a promise. Both offer clarity and the authentic basis to move forward, even if there is no place to go at the moment. Lip service is another story. Nothing kills democracy or transformation faster than lip service. The future does not die from opposition; it disappears in the face of lip service.

The key distinction is between commitment and barter, but what is most dangerous to commitment is lip service. Lip service sabotages commitment. It offers an empty step forward. It comes in the form of "I'll try." It is an agreement made standing next to the exit door. Whenever someone says they will try hard, agree to think about it, or do the best they can, it is smart to consider that statement a no. It may not be a final refusal, but at that moment there is no commitment. We can move forward with refusal; we cannot move forward with maybe. Trying hard is just a coded refusal. Whether lip service is a response to feeling coerced, to a sense of internal obligation, or to just a desire to look good, it is really a way to escape the moment, and it hijacks commitment.

Wholehearted commitment makes a promise to peers about our contribution to the success of the whole. It is centered in two questions: "What promise am I willing to make?" and "What is the price I am willing to pay for the success of the whole effort?" It is a promise for the sake of a larger purpose, not for the sake of personal return. Commitment comes dressed as a promise.

Another key is to see the importance of the words "a promise to peers." More on this later, but peers receive the promises and determine whether the promises are enough to bring an alternative future into existence. Enough to care for the common good. The convener's task is to direct the eyes and words of citizens toward each other. That is why we have people sit in circles, facing one another.

What reassures us in this process is that we need the commitment of much fewer people than we thought to create the future we have in mind.

The Questions for the Conversation for Commitment

Commitment embraces two kinds of promises:

- Promises about my behavior and actions with others
- Promises about results and outcomes that occur in the world

As suggested earlier, promises that matter are those made to peers, not those made to people who have power over us (parents, bosses, leaders). The future is created through the exchange of promises between citizens, the people with whom we have to live out the intentions of the change. It is to these people that we give our commitments, and it is they who decide if our offer is enough—for the person, for the institution, for the community. Peers have the right to declare that the promise made is not enough to serve the interests of the whole. As in each act of refusal, this is the beginning of a longer conversation.

Promises are sacred. They are the means by which we choose accountability. We become accountable the moment we make our promises public.

Depending on our taste and intuition, here is a menu of questions for this conversation:

What promises am I willing to make?

What measures have meaning to me?

What price am I willing to pay?

What is the cost to others for me to keep my commitments, or to fail in my commitments?

What is the promise I'm willing to make that constitutes a risk or major shift for me?

What is the promise I am postponing?

What is the promise or commitment I am unwilling to make?

If you really want to ground this conversation, write the promises by hand, and sign and date them. Then collect and publish the whole set. About once a quarter, meet and ask, "How's it going?"

A note: "I am willing to make no promise at this moment" is a fine and acceptable stance. It is a commitment of another kind. Saying "I pass" is an act of citizen refusal that is ennobling. This means that refusal does not cost someone their membership in the circle. We need to hold the space for that kind of refusal. When we honor the refusal of one person, we honor that choice for all persons. When one person says no, that person is speaking in some way for all of us. Holding space for refusal in the midst of a conversation for commitment gives depth and substance to the choice or commitment all others have made.

The only act that puts membership at risk is the unwillingness to honor our word. This is the choice to not fulfill our promises or not retract them when we know they will not be fulfilled. Refusing to make a promise is an act of integrity and supports community. Not being a person who honors their word by either fulfilling their promises or retracting when we know they will not be fulfilled sabotages community, and it does not matter what the excuse. This is the bloody trail of lip service.

Conversation Six: Gifts

In our attraction to problems, deficiencies, disabilities, and needs, the missing community conversation is about gifts. The only cultural practices that focus on gifts are retirement parties and funerals. We only express gratitude for your gifts when you are on your way out or gone. If we really want to know what gifts others see in us, we have to wait for our own eulogy, and even then, as the story goes, we will miss it by a few days.

In community building, rather than focusing on our deficiencies and weaknesses, which will most likely not go away, we gain more leverage when we focus on the gifts we bring, and seek ways to capitalize on them. Instead of problematizing people and work, the conversation that searches for the mystery of our gifts brings the greatest change and results. This is especially true when caring for or acting with people who live in exile. The other. Low-performing employees, low-income people, people with disabilities, people with the law against their side, family members who are hard to reach and show up late at Thanksgiving and are vegetarians.

The focus on gifts confronts people with their essential core, that which has the potential to make the difference and change lives for good. This resolves the unnatural separation between work and life. Who we are at work is our life. Who we are in life is our work. The leadership task—indeed the task of every citizen—is to bring the gifts of those on the margin into the center. This applies to each of us as an individual, for our life work is to bring our gifts into the world. This is a core quality of a hospitable community, whose work is to bring into play the gifts of all its members, especially strangers.

The Gifts Distinctions

Authentically acknowledging our gifts is what it means to be inclusive or to value diversity. Judith Snow, a powerful voice in the disabilities world, declared that the purpose of her life was to eliminate the language of disabilities from our vocabulary. She stated in an email to me, "My deepest desire is to make the world safe for people whose abilities and contributions are generally unrecognized." She created a world where no one is known by, is labeled with, or takes his identity from his disabilities, only from his gifts. This is in no way a denial of our limitations, just a recognition that they are not who we are. I am not what I am not able to do. I am what I am able to do—my gifts and capacities. Judith was a person who had control of her mind, her voice, and her fingers. She was supposed to die as a teenager, but chose to go in her sixties. Still too soon.

The point is that an alternative future, and the community that ushers it in, come into being when we capitalize on our gifts and capacities. Bringing the gifts of those on the margin into the center is a primary task of leadership and citizenship.

The distinction here is straightforward, between gifts and deficiencies.

When we look at deficiencies, we strengthen them. What you see is what you get. When you label or name me arrogant or quietly aggressive, or remote and homeless, which I am, that is what you are going to get. In this way, the focus on gifts is a practical stance, not a moral one. What do you want from me—my deficiencies or my capacities?

The Gifts Questions

The gifts conversation boils down to our willingness to stop telling people about

> What they need to improve
>
> What didn't go well
>
> How they should do it differently next time

Instead, confront them with their gifts. Talk to others about

> The gifts you've received from them
>
> The unique strength that you see in them
>
> The capacities they have that bring something unique and needed in the world
>
> What they did in the last ten minutes that made a difference

Gifts of This Gathering

Every time we gather, there needs to be space for a discussion of what gifts have been exchanged. This question needs to be asked of the community:

> **What gift have you received from another in this room?** Tell the person in specific terms.

We focus on gifts because what we focus on, we strengthen. The gifts-of-this-gathering question can be asked this way:

> **What has someone in your small group done today that has touched you or moved you or been of value to you?**

or

> **In what way did a particular person engage you in a way that had meaning?**

In practical terms, this means that in each small group, one person at a time tells the others what they have received and appreciated from others.

Because we are so awkward about this kind of discussion, the conversation needs to be set up in a special way. We ask the person who hears about what they have given another to say, "Thank you; I like hearing that." We want to let the statements of gifts have a chance to sink in. Help people put aside the routine of deflecting the appreciation and denying their gifts. Encourage them not to say that others brought it out of them, or what a great group this is, or how they got lucky for once and will try to not let it happen again.

This means we enforce a complete ban on denying gifts and discussing weaknesses and what is missing. No human problem solving allowed. Often, because they have been so conditioned by the retributive culture that we have experienced, people want negative feedback. This is packaged in the name of learning and growth.

Don't buy the packaging. The longing for feedback that we can "work on" is really a defense against the terrible burden of acknowledging our gifts and getting about the work of living into them, which we can call "fulfilling our destiny"—language so demanding and imposing, no wonder I would rather keep swimming in the morass of my needs and incompleteness. Save me from constructive feedback. I can stand most of the time; I don't need reconstruction. Eye contact will do.

> Among all the things which God created in His universe, He created nothing that is useless. He created the snail as a cure for a wound, the fly as a cure for the sting of the wasp, the gnat as a cure for the bite of the serpent, the serpent as a cure for a sore, and the spider as a cure for the sting of a scorpion.
>
> Shabbat 77b, Babylonian Talmud, from *Judaism and Social Justice*, by Harriet Kaufman

The Gift Each Brings to the World

Beyond the conversation about what gifts occurred in this gathering, we each have to deal with the extent that we are bringing the gifts given to us at birth or beyond into the world. We are aware of our deficiencies beyond belief or utility. What we are blind to are our gifts, the ones unique to us. These are qualities we have not earned but that have come to us as an act of grace. Our work in life is to know and accept these gifts, for acceptance is what is required to bring them forth.

The questions to ask are the following:

What is the gift you currently hold in exile?

What is it about you that no one knows about?

What are you grateful for that has gone unspoken?

What is the positive feedback you receive that still surprises you?

What is the gift you have that you do not fully acknowledge?

As with all the conversations, there may be no immediate and clear answers to these questions. That doesn't matter. The questions themselves work on us, and when they are asked, this work is activated. In the asking, we are creating space for gifts, which are central to restoration, restoration that wants to occur at this moment. In this way, the questions are the transformation, simply by being named.

The Questions at a Glance

The heart of the conversations emerging from all of these questions is to create a sense of belonging with others and also a sense of accountability for oneself and care for the commons.

Here is a summary of the core questions associated with each conversation:

What is the choice you made by being here? (Invitation)

How much risk do you plan to take, and how participative do you plan to be in this gathering or project? (Ownership)

What are the crossroads you/we are at that are appropriate to the purpose of the gathering? (Possibilities)

What declarations are you prepared to make about the possibilities for the future? (Possibilities)

To what extent do you see yourself as cause of the problem you are trying to fix? (Ownership)

What is the story you hold about this community or this issue, and what are the payoffs and costs of this story? (Ownership)

What are your doubts and reservations? (Dissent)

What is the yes you no longer mean? (Dissent)

What promises are you willing to make to your peers? (Commitment)

What gifts have you received from each other? (Gifts)

> When a child is born, they are bringing a gift from the spirit world that the community needs.
>
> Sobonfu

The important thing about these questions is that they name the agenda that can shift the nature of the future. They are a curriculum for restorative community. The power is in the asking, not in the answers. And we do not have to get it just right. There are many ways to frame the questions, as long as we do not make the way too easy. The work is to invent questions that fit the business you are up to and the conditions you are attempting to shift.

A final caveat. These ideas and methodology depend on a certain amount of goodwill. When individuals or communities are more committed to being right than to creating an alternative future, then nothing we do can make much of a difference. There are those times and places where the cynicism, despair, and resignation run so deep that all that we attempt seems to fall on deaf ears. In the long run, I do not believe this is ever the case. But there are moments, specific gatherings, that just do not go well. At these times, all we can do is forgive ourselves for how little difference we seem to have made and then perhaps have a conversation with God.

CHAPTER 13

Bringing Hospitality into the World

We usually associate hospitality with a culture, a social practice, a more personal quality to be admired. In Western culture, where individualism and security seem to be priorities, we need to be more thoughtful about how to bring the welcoming of strangers into our daily way of being together.

• • •

The six conversations have power when they occur in a context of hospitality. Here are the design elements for structuring hospitality into our gatherings.

Welcome and Greeting

Everything counts. We take our cues from the hospitality industry, especially from good restaurants and hotels. Greet people at the door; welcome them personally and help them get seated. Introduce them to some people whom they do not know. People enter in isolation. Reduce the isolation they came with; let them know they came to the right place and are not alone.

Example: Carlsbad, California

When Ray Patchett, city manager of Carlsbad, California, decided to involve the community in determining its future, he and his staff placed a red carpet from the street to the front door of the meeting place. They had people at the door to welcome people and escort them to the meeting room. In the meeting room, each citizen was personally introduced to other citizens. A local group was playing music; light food was offered. Photos taken by children were on the wall. Get the picture? When you came to this meeting, you knew you had come to the right place. Of course this took some time and effort on the part of the city manager team, but what a message of care and inclusion for the citizens of Carlsbad.

Restate the Invitation

After the welcome, begin with a statement of why you are there. Declare the possibility that led to the invitation. Use everyday language and speak from the heart, without PowerPoint presentations, slides, video, and so on. Use words and phrases that express choice, faith, willingness to act, commitment to persevere, and the fact that the leaders came to listen, not just to speak.

Connection Before Content

Before diving into the agenda, citizens need to be connected to one another. Whenever we enter a room, we do so with doubt and still attached to wherever we just came from. Connecting citizens to each other is not intended to be just an icebreaker, which is fun yet does little to break the isolation or create community. Icebreakers will achieve contact, but not connection. Connection occurs when we speak of what matters about this moment. This is done most easily through questions (surprise!).

Some examples of connection questions:

What led you to accept the invitation?

Why was it important for you to be here today?

What is the price others paid for you to be here?

If you could invite someone from your life, past or present, to sit beside you and support you in making this meeting successful, who would that be?

Since connection occurs most easily in small face-to-face groupings, create circles of three or six. Request that people sit with those they know the least; this gives each person the freedom to be who they truly are and not who their colleagues think they should be. It also symbolizes the intent to have people move beyond the boundaries of their own history and alliance.

Certain groupings are better for learning and connection; others are better for closure and problem solving. Use a diverse mix of people, people who know each other the least, early in the gathering. This "maximum mix" is good for opening questions and raising doubts. Use affinity groupings, composed of those who are most familiar with each other, for planning actions and making promises.

One structural sequence for creating community is to start with the individuals reflecting on the question and then have them talk in trios, next in groups of six, and then to the whole community. Shorthand is 1-3-6-all. If you are short on time, groups of three are ideal. No place to hide in a threesome.

Late Arrivals

Someone always comes late, especially in community work. This does not mean we do not start on time, but the fact that a person showed up needs to be acknowledged. Welcome them without humiliation and connect them with the group. Restored community is created when every gathering is a demonstration of the future we came to create, so we need to take a moment to include those who come late. This is a defining feature of a culture of hospitality, and taking the time to welcome a latecomer sets the tone for what we consider to be important, which is relatedness.

Early Departure

When a participant leaves early, there is a hole and a kind of emptiness left behind. The early exit leaves a void in the community. It hurts the community; there is a cost, a consequence to the community. This takes energy and resources from the gathering and represents a cost to the experience of community and belonging.

People will leave early, usually for good reason, so no need to take it personally, but good reason to take this seriously. Loss is an element of engagement. The way we treat the loss of a member is as important as the way we treat the welcome and the conclusion of the gathering. Here is a way to handle early departures that reflects that spirit:

Ask in the beginning for people to give notice of leaving. Ask them to leave in public, not to sneak out in the dark of night or in silence or during a break.

Acknowledge their leaving in a deliberate way.

Have them announce to the group that they are leaving and where they are going. This will create some discomfort, but that is the nature of separation.

When they get up to leave, have three people from the group say, "Here's what you've given us . . ." This is a moment for the gifts conversation.

Ask the soon-to-be-departed, "What are you taking with you? What shifted for you, became clearer? What value have you received as a result of being here? Is there anything else you'd like to say to the community?"

Thank them for coming.

Remove their chairs—if the chairs remain empty, we are only reminded of our loss.

All of this takes time, but we are choosing depth over speed. Plus, how we treat these people today is how we will be treated tomorrow.

Breaking Bread Together

In creating the conversation and social space that support community, we need to address another dimension of welcome, one that has traditionally defined culture: food. It brings the sacred into the room. It is the symbol of hospitality. Providing food is as direct as we can be in performing a life-giving act. When we take it seriously, we know how to do this right. What is needed is consciousness about having food and about what kind of food fits our intention.

One small request: Most food served in meetings is about satiation, not health. Even in health care settings or meetings about creating healthy communities, we serve pastries, cookies, fast food, chips, pretzels. This is not food; it is fuel and habit that are nutritionally and environmentally unconscious.

Let there be apples so that we have some way of moving beyond the illusion of paradise; grapes for the sake of pleasure; bread, unleavened if you can find it, a reminder of the Sabbath . . . you get the point. Natural, healthy food, prepared by local merchants. Food that reflects the diversity of the world we are embracing. Grown within fifty miles of our gathering place to reduce the carbon footprint.

Some people will complain. Let them.

CHAPTER 14

Designing Physical Space That Supports Community

Physical space is more decisive in creating community than we realize. Most meeting spaces are designed for control, negotiation, and persuasion. Although the room itself is not going to change, we always have a choice about how we rearrange and occupy whatever room we are handed. Community is built when we sit in circles, when there are windows and the walls have signs of life, when every voice can be equally heard and amplified, when we all are on one level— and the chairs have wheels and swivel.

When we have an opportunity to design new space, the same communal consciousness applies. We need reception areas that tell us we are in the right place and are welcome, hallways wide enough for intimate seating and casual contact, eating spaces that refresh us and encourage relatedness, rooms designed with nature, art, conviviality, and citizen-to-citizen interaction in mind. And we need large community spaces that have those qualities of great communal intimacy.

Finally, the design process itself needs to be an example of the future we are intending to create. The material and built world is a reflection of the connectedness, openness, and curiosity of the group gathered to design the space. Authentic citizen engagement is as important as design expertise.

• • •

The discussion to this point has been about creating a new communal conversation by redesigning the social space within which we gather. There is one more aspect of conversation that is important to creating the experience of community and belonging: this is to be intentional about how we design and occupy physical space.

The Physical Space

The room has importance beyond its functionality. Every room we occupy serves as a metaphor for the larger community that we want to create. This is true socially and also physically. The room is the visible expression of today's version of community or lack of it. The room we are in, and how we choose to occupy it, is what we have to work with in the present moment. If the future we desire does not exist in this room, today, then it will never occur tomorrow. This is what is meant by "Change the room, change the culture."

Meeting rooms are traditionally designed for efficiency, control, and business as we know it.

Conference rooms have long rectangular tables basically designed for negotiation, one side facing the other. The effect is that you can only see those on "the other side." You sit blind to those on your own side of the table. So here we are, gathering to build community, accountability, and relatedness, yet unable to make eye contact with half the people in the room.

The ends of the table are VIP positions. We all know this and avoid these seats. They are most often occupied last. In a restaurant, the person at the end of the table usually ends up paying the bill, so who wants to sit there by choice? This is also the typical design for boardrooms, which are all about prestige, privilege, and control.

Auditoriums are designed for citizens to passively receive what others have produced. They are great for presentation and performance, which leaves the audience with their backs turned to each other, all eyes facing front.

Classrooms are mostly designed for instruction. The usual layout says there will be one expert who knows, ten to three hundred students who are there to absorb what the expert knows. Structured for teaching, not learning. This arrangement gives little recognition to the importance of peer-to-peer learning. Sometimes we see the hollow square or U-shaped arrangement of tables and chairs. Same problem: each person loses sight of one-third to one-quarter of the people in the room, and those we can see are on the other side of a moat of empty space.

Reception areas are mostly designed for security. The message is that you have to demonstrate your right to enter this building. Hardly the welcome that encourages belonging. If you want to see a reception area designed for welcoming and hospitality, visit a nice hotel, a bar, or a good restaurant. The best business reception area I have seen is at LivePerson, a tech company for which I have great affection. You walk in the door and you are in a kitchen and eating area. The kitchen is the traditional center of warmth and relationship in any house or institution. Placing it right up front says, "Welcome, you belong here, have some fruit or snacks." Brilliant.

Hallways are designed for transportation. There are a growing number of community-conscious buildings that create hallways as city streets—places where casual contact is valued, the rooms you pass have internal windows like storefronts, and the hallway is wide enough for sitting areas. All created to bring life to our experience.

Cafeterias are often designed as efficient refueling stations. The concern seems to be how many people we can feed and how quickly. Chairs, tables, walls, and food stations are set up for efficiency, easy maintenance, don't linger, please get back to work. As if sitting and being with other employees is not work. There was a time when there were executive dining rooms and employee dining rooms. There may be reasons for the separation by rank and status, though none come to mind at the moment. Where these still exist, the resolution is to decorate the employee eating area as nicely as the space for executives.

Bring the Room to Life and Life to the Room

Although we may not have control over the form and shape of the room, we always have choices about how to occupy the room. The task is to rearrange the room to meet our intention to build relatedness, accountability, and commitment. This puts the convener in the role of interior designer. I spend my life being neurotically fussy about what room to meet in, and how to rearrange it once I get there. This is embarrassing and awkward, earns me weird looks, and receives irrational refusals, and sometimes I just get tired lugging chairs around the room. But this is work that has to be done in a world not designed for human interaction.

The room needs to express the quality of aliveness and belonging that we wish for the community. Here is what this entails:

Arrange the Room as the Shape of Things to Come

The circle is the geometric symbol for community, and therefore for arranging the room. No tables if possible. If tables are a given, then choose round ones (the shape of communion), which are better than rectangles (the shape of negotiation), or classroom-style tables (the shape of instruction). If tables are a given, find the smallest ones you can.

The ideal seating for a small group is a circle of chairs with no table. Put the chairs as close together as possible, which forces people to lean in to one another. People will complain that they have no place to put their laptop or water. They have laps and the floor. The circle with no table instantly and visually communicates to citizens or employees that dialogue and relationship with each other are as important as any content to be covered.

Pick a Room with a View

A room without windows blocks out the larger world that we are attempting to care for. A room with no windows carries the message that the larger world does not, for this moment, exist. It isolates us from that larger world and gives permission to be focused narrowly on the smaller world within the boundaries of our own interests. It makes the neighborhood, the city, and the globe invisible. It also keeps the energy produced by our gathering trapped in too small a space. There is no exchange of energy between our work and the world when we are trapped in a box.

Welcome Nature into the Room

Gather near a window, if there is one. Open the curtains; pull up the shades or blinds. If there is too much light to see the PowerPoint presentation, so be it. Perhaps there is a message in this.

Bring in plants, even if they are artificial. As my friend Allan Cohen says, artificial plants are real: they are real plastic. The walls and furnishings of most of our meeting places are dead. The spaces are designed in the name of modernity, efficiency, and low maintenance. We do not have to passively acquiesce to this.

Even one candle or one flower in the room changes everything. They completely understand this in India.

Amplify the Whole Room

All voices need to be heard equally, and we have the technology to amplify a whole room. Look at a concert hall if you doubt this. As mentioned earlier, never have one microphone on a stand that people must line up to use. This breeds citizen speeches, gives too much power to the extremes, and reinforces the power imbalance between leader/expert and follower. Having three handheld mics that can move around the room works much better.

Example: Conservation Commissioner

I met a conservation commissioner in Colorado who was constantly arbitrating disputes between ranchers, farmers, environmentalists, loggers, and all who care about our open spaces. He decided to buy a van and amplification equipment so that wherever in the state he went, he could mic the room. All could speak without walking up to a podium or lectern, and all could be heard equally. He said that as soon as he made this investment, the tone of the conversations shifted. The differences did not go away, but the contentiousness of the debate subsided, and civility and respect increased.

Choose Chairs That Swivel
and Have Wheels and Low Backs

A chair is not just for support; it is also a means of mobility and transportation. Most meeting-room chairs are designed for straight lines and stability. If you place them in circles and move too much, they get nervous and unhappy.

If designed well, a chair can encourage movement from one small group to another. It can facilitate moving our attention back and forth from our small group to the larger forum. A movable chair is a metaphor for the ability to move back and forth from the concern for local tribal integrity and the needs of the whole.

A swivel chair tells us that we must keep rotating to take in all that is around us so that what we create in our own unit or neighborhood occurs in the context of a larger world. Wheels allow us to move among small groups easily. If there are wheels on the chair, they ask to be used and serve to convince us that we are at every moment connected and willing to travel to all else that is happening in the room.

Level the Playing Field

Rooms in public buildings, presumably designed for civic dialogue, often have a stage or raised platform. A platform or stage creates a demand for performance and judgment; it looks like the throne of the monarch, the bench of the judge. This is not the arrangement for democracy or community. Granted, watching a stage together gives us a common experience, but it does not connect citizens to each other. When we watch the stage together, we have once again turned our backs on each other. This obliterates the circle, the traditional shape of community.

The raised platform, besides underlining the superiority of a few raised higher than the heads of many others, distorts the need for dialogue by encouraging questions and answers. It's as if citizens can show up only with questions, and the leaders will be the ones with the answers. Question-and-answer sessions are patriarchy's answer to interaction.

Most city councils operate from raised platforms that isolate elected officials from citizens. Those platforms are effective in establishing the authority of the leaders and good for creating order. They are weak in creating a structure in which the leaders themselves are physically set up to work well together. Plus the leader who would declare to citizens, "We want your input," and do this while looking down on them—from behind a big table, sitting on a plush chair, speaking into his own microphone—makes the intention impossible to implement. In these situations, the leader is as imprisoned by the structure as the citizen.

Even in the theater, which is traditionally all about performance, there are structures designed to reduce the social and emotional distance between actor and audience. Theaters in the round put the stage in the center of the space so that the audience becomes a participant in the drama.

Bring in Art and the Aesthetic

This is a larger conversation than can be dealt with here, but here is the gist of it: There can be no transformation without art. Art in the form of theater, poetry, music, dance, literature, painting, and sculpture. Communities by and large know this and invest heavily in the arts. Those who want to heal the wounds of a fragmented community initiate hundreds of art projects for those living on the margin. Art brings these voices into the mainstream. Most communities are proud of their arts tradition and rightly so.

If this is true for our larger communities, then it must be present each time we gather.

Why would we assemble without a moment of silence, a song, a recitation? We often have this consciousness in education, workshops, and conferences. This sensibility should not be sequestered into those special occasions but be a part of our daily life. If every gathering is an occasion for producing for ourselves a future we want to inhabit, then we need to design it for that intention, and we need art to accomplish this.

If it is a large gathering, invite a local band or choir or dance troupe to welcome people into the session. Each time you break and reconvene, create some form of art or inspiration to mark the transition. Read a poem, or take a moment to create a poem, write in a journal, breathe together. This is all very doable with little cost or preparation.

Every group of twenty people has someone who would be willing to sing a song, recite a poem, or tell a story. All we need to do is make the request at the beginning of the gathering, and as people come to trust each other, someone will offer their gift of song, poem, or story to the community. When this happens, the tone in the room shifts, and the place becomes a little more sacred.

Put Life on the Wall

There is nothing as lonely as an empty wall. Our halls and meeting spaces are filled with empty walls. Interestingly, this is not true of executive offices or spaces designed for sales presentations. Great attention is paid to making these places warm and welcoming. Art collections adorn the walls, seating is comfortable, and windows are softened with fabric. Granted, this decoration serves as a sign of privilege and importance, but it is a good thing. Why not extend this symbolism to those spaces where citizens and employees gather?

"An empty wall is a testimony to the insignificance of the human spirit," observed pioneering street life researcher William H. Whyte. Our job is to affirm the significance of the human spirit, and filling the walls with photos and with art by citizens, youth, and employees is very doable. The library or art galleries in the community would be willing to curate public space. They do it frequently for restaurants and shops. It is not a question of cost; it is a question of consciousness.

At the end of the day, we have to ask, how can we create aliveness when the wall sits sadly empty?

Design and Build Opportunities

Every once in a while, there comes an opportunity to work with architects to design new spaces that support community. These are rare moments (unless you are an architect) when we can bring a communal consciousness to the construction of a new building or the rehabilitation of an old one.

An elegant quote from Christopher Alexander in Book 1 of his *Nature of Order* series reminds us how rare and powerful these opportunities are to bring a new consciousness into the material world:

> Common sense tells us—or seems to tell us—that the physical environment affects our lives. It has often been said, certainly, that the shape of buildings affects our ability to live, our well-being, perhaps our behavior. Winston Churchill is believed to have said, "we shape our buildings; and they shape us." But *how* do they affect us?
>
> I shall argue that the geometry of the physical world—its space—has the most profound impact possible on human beings: it has impact on the most important of all human qualities, our inner freedom, or the sense of life each person has. It touches on internal freedom, freedom of the spirit.
>
> I shall argue that the right kind of physical environment, when it has living structure, nourishes freedom of the spirit in human beings. In the wrong kind, lacking living structure, freedom of the spirit can be destroyed or weakened. If I am right, this will suggest that the character of the physical world has impact on possibly the most precious attribute of human existence. It is precisely life—the living structure of the environment—which has *this* effect.

Later he summarizes by stating, "In an environment which has living structure, each of us tends, more easily, to become alive."

As mentioned earlier, the architecture of a building can support a community of belonging in the design of its walls, ceilings, hallways, reception areas, training and community rooms, eating spaces, meeting rooms, accommodations for food, breakout areas, and small gathering spaces. This does not even get into the design of work spaces, which I am not dealing with, as it is such well-covered territory.

The distinction to be made here is between great design and modernist aesthetic design that is about modernity, newness, and placing an architectural and landscape footprint that produces a legacy, which is more about the architect than the neighborhood. These modernist places are usually indifferent or strictly utilitarian with respect to human habitation. Michael Freedman, an urban architect and planner, can show award-winning building designs that no one wants to inhabit and award-winning landscape designs that keep people from congregating and have no relationship to their neighborhood. This is a stunning reality. How could we design buildings and communal spaces that are not friendly to their inhabitants? Not so stunning perhaps when you realize that we design institutions, social structures, and gatherings that have the same effect.

Here is the bigger point. The buildings and material forms that we create are an outgrowth of our social fabric and capacity to be in community together. They have a powerful impact on our experience and relation to each other. Space matters.

Alienated and retributive cultures will create alienated and unfriendly buildings and public spaces. Patriarchal institutions will create physical space that glorifies those who lead them and the designers they choose, and they will be indifferent, in the name of cost, to the space dedicated to workers and citizens. This means we must be thoughtful about the quality of relatedness that exists among those designing our spaces: the owner and the architect. If neither is intentional about space and the neighborhood or place where it is located, and if their first priority is preeminence and branding, then we will continue to have instrumental spaces. These are spaces where conflicts are unresolved, isolation is taken for granted, and style conquers substance. We do have evidence that there is a choice.

Example: Citizen-Driven Design

Here is an example of how the planning process can involve citizens and increase the chances that the built environment will be friendly to community and belonging. In the world of community planning and landscape design, Ken Cunningham and his partner, John Spencer, have created a design process very much in line with the thinking offered here. They know that the quality of a plan is not just in the rightness of its design. The quality and success of a plan also depend on there being an authentic expression of the voices of the citizens who will occupy that space. The essence of Ken and John's process is to invite citizens to walk around, observe, and imagine what the space might become.

Every planning process claims to involve citizens and potential occupants, but in most cases it is lip service, holding to the belief that experts, usually from out of town, hold the real key to great design.

Ken and John treat citizens as producers of the design rather than as consumers who react and respond to the decisions of community leadership groups and planning experts.

The following are some elements of their thinking that fit well with the themes in this book:

- Ken and John work hard to get a cross section of people, especially those citizens who are typically disengaged. They actively recruit those on the margin and make sure they are welcome. They want two kinds of people in the room: those who have a direct stake in the design, whom they name the "internal community," and some outsiders, whom they call the "external supportive community." This recognizes that the wider community has a stake in the quality of design for each property or neighborhood. It takes a region to raise a property.

- Before citizens get involved in the design, Ken and John have them get to know each other. They have them meet in small groups and engage in many of the conversations for transforming community. In their groups, citizens talk about the crossroads facing this project, they discuss their doubts and reservations, and they hold the gifts conversation and name the promises they are willing to make to ensure that this project succeeds.

- Ken and John then identify several critical places in the property or neighborhood where the design will determine the essential experience of those who will eventually occupy the space. They have citizens physically walk these spots, and they have them ask themselves some interesting questions:
  - When I look at this spot, what do I see?
  - When I look, what do I know?
  - When I look, what are my assumptions?
  - When I look, what do I envision?

  These questions, asked early, evoke the imagination of those who will live with the design. This is different from creating designs or plans that express the imagination of the architect and developer.

- After the citizens have walked the physical spaces, Ken and John bring them together to post their answers to the questions. They are careful to record each comment exactly as spoken so that all ideas are held and documented. A primary goal is for citizens to recognize their contribution in the final plan. At each stage, Ken and John can point to the language and words that came from citizens.

It is after the conversation with citizens that Ken and John do the traditional research and define the core elements and requirements facing the design.

Citizens are then brought together again and presented with an organized version of their comments and the results of the research. In this meeting, Ken and John use some creative ways to sustain ownership and commitment:

- In small groups they use a talking stick, which ensures that every person's voice is heard and prevents the more verbal people from dominating the conversation.

- They have designed a physical game in which people can explore and discover their choices. People place objects, buildings, benches, parks, and all the other design specifics on the board and then talk through the trade-offs in the design process. Experts usually do this; here, citizens do it.

When strong differences become obvious, they also handle conflict in a special way. They avoid the arbitrator role and instead use a fishbowl structure to resolve conflicts. They put those who disagree in the center of a group and have chairs for others to occupy so that their voices can be heard. This means that other citizens participate in conflict resolution instead of the usual approach of handing the issue to a professional.

When people get stuck in their differences, Ken intervenes. He tells them, and other citizens who are interested, that they have twenty minutes to resolve the conflict. At the end of the time, Ken comes over with a pink pearl or a silver dagger. One of the two is placed on the design, depending on whether the citizens have been able to reach agreement. If they can agree, they get the pink pearl. If not, a silver dagger is placed on the design and the group moves on. He reports that this structure often achieves agreement, even when people have been at odds with each other for years.

The simple but elegant device of Ken and John's game keeps citizens engaged and treats each design question as a challenge that the community has the capacity to resolve. It also moves differences from an abstract discussion of beliefs to concrete and certain terms on paper, which is cheap.

The final step is to document what has been developed in a draft design, which is presented back to the citizens. They gather to review the design and experience the product of their efforts.

This approach is such a radical and elegant expression of common sense. As you know, in the traditional planning process, experts do most of the work. Citizens are usually asked what they want in the design, and then the experts come up with a draft design that is presented to the citizens for feedback. The experts take the feedback back to their office and prepare a final design, which is then proposed to decision makers. There is little attention paid to creating more relatedness among stakeholders. There is no structure to have conflicts resolved by the advocates themselves. Making sure that citizens can identify where their own ideas show up in the design is left to chance.

The real difference between what Ken and John do and what is traditionally done is really a contrast between the contexts out of which designers operate. Ken and John bring a context of valuing the gifts of citizens, understanding the importance of engagement, and appreciating the hospitality of physical space, all elements of restorative places.

There Is More Than Enough Time and Just Enough Money

A final comment on space: Cost and speed are always cited in the argument against great design, but the discussion about cost and speed is not really about cost and speed. It is part of an agenda which declares that human experience is a low priority. The argument against the importance of the aesthetic is an argument against human freedom. Low-cost and quickly constructed buildings and spaces become warehouses designed to keep under one roof and under control those people whom we do not value. We measure their value in dollars and efficiency. We have too often seen the construction of ugly spaces and buildings in the name of cost reduction or of saving taxpayers' dollars. It is not about the money. When a hallowed institution like a sports franchise or a large employer threatens to move out of town, we have all the money that is needed.

Don't ever take at face value the argument about no funds and no time. Our stance about cost and speed is simply a measure of our commitment. In every case, low cost and fast action are really an argument against the dignity of citizens and against a more democratic and humanly inclusive process.

As a final thought, I want to acknowledge that the struggle to find or adapt space to support citizens facing each other with no barriers in between is an unending quest. The most sophisticated designs—whether for offices, museums, or public buildings—still want rooms with long rectangular tables, or seats and pews nailed to the floor facing forward, or cameras and microphone taking precedence over eye contact. This struggle is also an internal one, as I wonder whether getting people out of the pews, out of the bolted-down seats, or away from the comfortable conference setup is worth the disruption. The wish to be approved of or just to take the easier way is endlessly appealing. The temptation to just let the world sit where they want and stay disconnected always raises the question of my own intention, my own commitment, my own resignation. Each time I yield to that temptation, it is always a mistake. Sorry.

CHAPTER 15

The End of
Unnecessary Suffering

There is a future that I know to be possible.

As is often said, you only teach what you need to learn, so it is my own desire for community, my own sense of isolation and unbelonging that have driven me into the work that has led to this book. Much of my life has been lived on the margin, outside of community, so I have firsthand familiarity with the toll it takes on a human being. This began so long ago that I have only a dim memory of its ever being any other way. Besides, any explanation I come up with would only be my story. Fiction it is. Over the last fifteen years, I have tiptoed cautiously, even reluctantly, toward fuller membership and belonging in the place where I reside, Cincinnati.

The possibility that is working on me is the reconciliation of community. Reconciliation is for me the possibility of the end of unnecessary suffering. This is the context within which I show up, even though, as with us all, I sometimes don't know whether I am working for God or the devil.

As I work to create the reconciliation and end to suffering that I am committed to, the extent of the pain running through our communities keeps commanding my attention. I want to make a distinction about this pain: it is the difference between human and political suffering. Human suffering is the pain that is inherent in being alive: isolation, loneliness, illness, abandonment, loss of meaning, sadness, and finally (I think) death. These are unavoidable; they are going to happen to each of us, and try as we may, there is nothing we can do to prevent them. We have infinite choice in how to respond to this kind of human suffering, but it is part of the deal and is what gives vitality, meaning, and texture to a life.

The other kind of pain is political suffering. This is avoidable and unnecessary suffering. Some of the avoidable suffering is very visible: poverty, homelessness, hunger, violence, the diaspora of those unable to return to their homeland, a deteriorated housing project, or a neighborhood in distress. There is also political suffering that is more subtle: people's learned dependency, internalized oppression, the absence of possibility, the powerlessness that breeds violence, imperialism, and a disregard for the worth of a human being. I am calling this political suffering because I believe it grows out of human choice: human choice to sustain a world of imbalance—surplus on one side and great scarcity on the other. This is a political choice, but not political in an electoral sense. It is not politics as in conservative or liberal, left or right. I am referring to politics as the choices we make about the distribution of power and control, and the mind-set that underlies those choices.

After all the social scientists, historians, economists, biologists, authors, and experts from all disciplines have finished with their explanations, it seems that what I am calling political, avoidable suffering occurs as a result of our disconnectedness and the imbalance of power and resources that is such a dominant feature of our culture. This in no way puts blame on anyone or any segment of society. I do not believe that "those people" exist anywhere in the world. I have simply come to believe that when we are unrelated to those whose lives are so different from ours, suffering increases.

When we see a growing distance between economic classes, an increase in protectionism and gatedness, and more resources coming into fewer hands, our capacity to value those exiled to the economic margin is reduced. This is not just about large societal movements; it is also about our growing dependence on experts, our attraction to celebrity and power, our increasing tendency to label and come up with new diagnostic categories in which to pour more services. All of this is rationalized in the name of cost control and greater expertise. These are what I consider the real politics of our lives. Where does choice reside, who decides, and at what moment is the interest of the larger whole given voice?

• • •

The political suffering will decrease as we collectively choose to be together in a way that creates a space for something new to occur. What is needed is for us to choose over and over to more widely distribute ownership and accountability. These choices will spring from the hands of citizens, rather than the hands of experts, leaders, and system executives. These choices will arise when we value, invest in, and recognize the gifts and capacities of citizens.

We have evidence that this is possible and that it works. If you are doubtful, look at all the research on what constitutes a high-performing team; examine the employee involvement and customer service movement of the 1980s and early 1990s and how it helped bring US companies back from the edge of irrelevance. Look at the decentralized operation of the megachurches of today and the way the armed services have long been interested in empowerment and point-of-contact decision making. In each of these efforts, existing leadership took the initiative, and citizens and employees and members accepted their role in producing an alternative future.

Therefore, consider how shifting our thinking and practice concerning the politics of experience could achieve reconciliation in several dimensions of community that are sources of so much grief.

Youth

Youth are a unifying force in community. Hard to argue against the next generation. An alternative future opens when we shift our view of youth (say, fourteen- to twenty-four-year-olds) from problem to possibility, from deficiency to gift. When you drive by a street corner and see young people hanging out at odd hours making a living in odd ways, you can view them as having gifts waiting to be given, rather than as being problems waiting to be solved.

If you notice that they are dealing drugs, you hold the thought that they have entrepreneurial skill; it is just aimed in the wrong direction. If you are concerned that they are not in school, well, they are learning something, just not what we had in mind.

Someone recently said that for youth who have dropped out of school and who have no support system around them, the street corner is the only classroom that welcomes them and is available to them. It has no entrance requirements and is open twenty-four hours a day. Is this way of thinking true? Not exactly, but it is useful because it puts us in a more forgiving stance.

If we care about youth instead of trying to control and inculcate them, then we have to deal with our adultism. This means we have to change the nature of our listening. Create places and people that welcome youth, where youth see themselves reflected in those who have chosen to work with them.

In a youth forum recently, ten young men in their late teens were asked if they knew a white person they could trust. One raised his hand. They were asked how many owned guns. You know the answer. How many had had a friend killed in the last two years? All raised their hands.

This reality most often leads to more conversations about programs on diversity, more action on weapons, or more vigilance. A new conversation would be to focus not on the suffering in their lives but on getting to know who these young men are, much as the Hoxseys and Sparoughs did in Findley House (described in chapter 8). To see them as gifts and capacities. These men (mostly) are entrepreneurial; they are leaders among their peers; they have a strong survival instinct; they are interesting and valuable human beings and have a hunger for this to be known about them. Let us just focus on that for a while and discover what emerges. Also, they are a reflection of the world we have helped create, so a conversation about our contribution to the plight of some of our youth would make a difference. This is not about guilt; it is about our accountability.

Public Safety

The shift is to believe that citizens have the capacity to create a safe neighborhood. It is street life and connected neighbors that make a neighborhood safe. We think the police can keep us safe. In our concern for safety, we too often defer to the professionals. Police are not the answer. They are needed for crime; they cannot produce safety.

There is in every neighborhood structures for citizens to volunteer: Citizens on Patrol, Neighborhood Watch, safety meetings, educational pamphlets hung on people's front doors by the police. These go under the title of crime prevention. Not so. They are an organized assault on the outside.

They are unkind to strangers hanging out in the neighborhood. Instead of making it possible for us to get to know who these human beings are, these structures embody the retributive mind-set.

The shift is to realize that safety occurs through neighborhood relatedness. The efforts that move in this direction focus on identifying neighborhood assets. On creating occasions for citizens to know each other through cleanup campaigns, block parties, and citizen activist movements to confront irresponsible landlords and abandoned houses and lots. Anything that helps neighbors know who lives on the street. Every neighborhood has certain connector people who know everyone else's goings-on. My street has Laura. She knows everyone; she is on the street all the time walking dogs, caring for animals regardless of

> Sidewalk contacts are the small change from which the wealth of public life may grow.
> Jane Jacobs

their owner, and generally providing the glue for all of us. She is the de facto mayor of Bishop Street. We need ways to recognize these people and others.

If we looked at the assets of the neighborhood, we would realize that youth are on the streets in the afternoon, and retired people and shut-ins have the time to watch what is going on. When we recognize the gifts of these people, safety will be produced.

Development
and the Local Economy

One of the largest divides in our cities is between the developers and the social activists. The activists want to protect the residents from their invested neighborhoods. They want to make sure that lower-income residents are not pushed out of their homes or their way of life. The developer community wants more home ownership and a lively area to attract young professionals and cultural creatives, empty nesters, gays, and lifestyle enthusiasts. The future is named development by the media and gentrification by the activists. This puts the social activists and the developers at odds with each other. The argument needs reframing. In most places, either the situation remains at an impasse, or the developers, with the help of local government and tax benefits from the federal government, carry the day.

It is a polarized conversation, with low trust and each side attached to its story. Developers bemoan the social services concentrated in poorer neighborhoods. Activists know that without a strong voice, the poor will be sent to warehouses under the interstate highway.

Reconciliation will occur through a new conversation in which the developers talk about the compassion they hold for those on the margin. The new conversation for the social activists is to acknowledge that without some wealth coming into their neighborhoods, they will continue to depopulate and deteriorate. The way into a different future is to build relatedness between these groups. Beneath their positions is a common concern for the well-being of the city. A perpetually wounded city serves no one. There are many examples of these groups coming together. It is all possible when people decide to work something out rather than trying to win and be right. It is the shift in conversation and a care for the whole that make the difference.

The other monster issue facing the country and community is the development of a local economy. Small businesses are the growth engine that is kind to community. Each neighborhood has a microeconomy that needs to be healthy. A place where people live, work, and shop. Most of the visible models are for well-off, resurgent neighborhoods. The emergent possibility is to create neighborhoods that are vital and friendly to the middle class. This is also the way out for those on the margin. For example, a strong local African American economy does more to create racial justice than minority hiring regulations and diversity workshops.

Jim Clingman, an active citizen of Cincinnati, has given voice to this issue for years. He calls it Blackonomics. Find his books and read them. He argues that the civil rights movement created political freedom for blacks to live, vote, and shop according to their wants, but this occurred at the expense of the economic well-being of African American small-business owners. This becomes the new conversation: how to marry capital with all the educational opportunities for creating business plans and incubator agencies that are intended to expand the pool of entrepreneurs. The answer for those on the margin is to become economically self-sufficient. Working at minimum-wage service jobs or becoming acculturated to work for mainstream large businesses leaves too many people outside the living-wage economy.

One more point. We need to educate people about the politics of the dollar. When they shop at the big-box stores, searching for the lowest cost, they do this at the expense of the community and local economy. For every dollar they save at the big boxes, they spend a dollar-fifty in taxes, high-interest loans for credit cards, overpriced staples at convenience stores, and get-me-through-the-night loan operations. Supporting small businesses, buying from those people who are a reflection of who you are, circulates money among businesses that will be ultimately sustaining. If we do not become conscious of the political and economic power of a single dollar, the class divide will only widen.

Family Well-Being and Human Services

In the human services world, we intend to approach families as whole systems; we talk about integrating service, but are so broken into disciplines and accreditations that it is mostly lip service. Even if we did organize services around the family, we are still deficiency oriented.

To fully explore this subject is beyond our purpose here, but a couple of headlines will make the point. The shift in framing is that people and families are a pool of gifts and capacities, not a series of needs and deficiencies. Their suffering is an effect of their isolation and their being labeled. The struggle in their life is to find a way to use their gifts. In the way we traditionally deliver service, by raising money for and valuing their deficiencies, we reflect and reinforce the cause of some of their troubles.

We still call citizens who seek help "cases." People who serve them are called "case workers." What does it mean when someone is labeled a "case"? By naming people cases, lawyers, social workers, human service workers in general dehumanize those they are committed to serve.

Human services also relate to citizens through diagnostic categories. We are interested only in their needs and deficiencies. We call people "homeless," "single mom," "poor," "ex-offender." If a family or person has no pressing needs and deficiencies, nothing that can be categorized, nothing that can be funded, we have no interest in that family or person. Perhaps we should develop diagnostic categories for people's gifts. Right now we have only crude positive labels: high school graduate, economic status, size of family, job experience. Suppose we named people in categories, using terms such as connector, knows everyone in the neighborhood, street-level entrepreneur, fashion plate, compassion for those in need, lights up a room when they enter, creative speech, practical intelligence, risk taker, cook.

The shift is to focus on gifts and capacities. Again, McKnight has led the way in this thinking.

Example: Cynthia Smith

Cynthia Smith was an assistant director of client services at the Hamilton County Department of Job and Family Services. They still "service" about thirty thousand citizens through the front door per month. Cynthia decided to work at shifting the thinking of her division from the needs of people to the gifts of people. She got interested in something called Appreciative Inquiry, which is a way of helping institutions build a future on what is positive about their past and present. It is designed to use appreciation as a form of leadership and organization development. According to some, this is a radical path for human services.

Cynthia also had the consciousness that the employees of Job and Family Services (JFS) reflect in their own lives the same struggles and heartaches of the general population that JFS is chartered to serve. This means that if we want to transform the context and thinking of those we are here to serve, then we must begin with ourselves. The internal culture of a human services system must value the gifts and capacities of its own employees before those employees can bring that mind-set to the community. People inside systems need to operate with compassion and appreciation toward each other. How can we be hospitable to the community if we are not hospitable to each other?

Another important step Cynthia took was to invite members of the community at large to be part of the internal conversations she initiated. She valued the capacity of the larger village to care for the success of JFS, an idea that is radical and healing in itself. Most government agencies think they have to defend and justify themselves to the community; Cynthia welcomed the community in, to help create an alternative and more restorative future. She believes that it does take a village to raise a child and was acting on it. Now, since this happened a while ago, some may ask, "Did it work?" "Was it cost effective?" "What evidence do we have about it?" Wrong questions. It for sure created for a moment in time an alternative culture and world. Proof enough.

Health Care

Health care ranks high on centralized control, private sector domination, and dependency on expert intervention. We thought that mergers and restructuring health care would help. We moved to managed care and brought 60 percent of the physicians under that umbrella. We privatized, with all the bottom-line efficiency that promised. We have invested heavily in research and dramatized the heroism of the professional. We market it on TV and billboards and with stories of the miracles of cure and science.

Health care also ranks high on every dimension for the conventional wisdom about how transformation occurs: strong leadership, noble vision, clear outcomes, predictable and regulated practices, tight measures, high-influence expertise, major investment in training.

So how is it going?

Not great. The United States spends 40 percent more on health care than the next highest spending nation, Switzerland. Yet the average rank in quality of care and health of citizens in the United States doesn't quite make it into the top ten.

What is paradoxical is that all who work in health care are committed, well-intentioned human beings. What is poignant is that most who work in the system, these committed, caring people, agree that the system is not working. Some call it broken.

For anything fundamental to change, the context needs to change. The current context is a conversation about better management, cost control, and universal access, called affordable care. This conversation is about minor improvements, making what is not working cheaper and more available. These conversations will not create an alternative future. To oversimplify, we are asking the wrong questions.

For example, the current conversation about controlling costs is not changing the nature of the system. A beginning conversation would be about who is responsible for our health.

Another example: We have only begun to shift to a focus on health versus disease. Slowly. The profession is very tentative about taking seriously nonchemical, nonsurgical forms of healing (which the profession would name as nonexpert intervention). In fact, any approach that focuses on anything other than system care, professional knowing, and chemical treatment is called alternative medicine. As if we would never turn to it first, only as an alternative. It is as if the conversation about prevention, widely available curatives, healthy eating, positive lifestyle habits, and ancient and traditional healing were not medicine but a second cousin. As if we had to choose between alternatives. Pick one or the other. And if you want your insurance company to pay for your getting healthy, you know which one gets the nod.

There are signs of a shift in context for health care. There is increasing evidence that if people are connected to their community and have people in their lives who care about their well-being—in other words, who experience a sense of belonging—they are healthier and live longer. These are encouraging indicators, although still outside the dominant conversation about the cost of professional services and who pays. Who is to say how this will eventually play out.

As for every other big question, there are small, local solutions occurring. Wherever you are, you can find examples of the future that you might seek. Someone, probably not too far away, is changing the world, though you will never see it in the news. Here are two examples of a major change in context in the realm of health care. These are two stories of individuals taking a stand for a possibility. They have organized their practice as an example of a future, and done so at significant personal cost, with the belief that local action, committed to over a long period of time, is what changes the world. And they do this in an industry where most feel helpless about anything really changing. Not these two.

Example: Paul Uhlig

A thoracic heart surgeon named Paul Uhlig is opening new possibilities for health care. In many ways, he is creating an alternative future for his calling.

He has been very innovative in the realm of collaborative care and the value of collaborative rounds. Collaborative rounds, in Paul's practice, are times when the physician, nurse, social worker, and other support people working with a patient literally stand in a circle with the patient and his or her family and talk together about the patient's condition and path of action. This means that decisions will be based on more than just the progress of the disease; they will include the viewpoints of the whole team, patient and family included. This is in sharp contrast to the common practice of placing the decisions about care in the hands of the single expert—the physician—or a team of experts. The idea that the patient, family, social workers, and nurses have a voice about care, expressed in front of all others, is a serious inversion of thinking. A shift from physician as the cause of care to the patient and care community. If you do not realize how radical this is, get thee to a hospital.

Collaborative care has been around for some time and was not invented by Paul and his team, but they have moved it forward with their advocacy. They have accumulated hard evidence of the impact of this kind of collaborative care, with data on the improvement in patient safety, length of stay in the hospital, patient and family satisfaction, and professional satisfaction. With the collaborative methodology, all these measures improve, at little increase in cost. If a drug were developed that produced even half of the outcomes that this innovation has produced, it would be used in every system in the country.

In the face of this, Paul has been treated by his industry as an interesting anomaly in the system. As a surgeon, he is near the top of the food chain. Still, wherever he goes, he both draws interest and catalyzes resistance.

The problem is that Paul's innovation confronts the dominance of the expert model in the extreme. And it delivers no large profits to the institution.

Paul believes that a community of care is what will make the difference in our health. Among his heart surgery patients, 95 percent will return to the lifestyle that broke their heart, after the professional supports, which are very expensive, have disappeared. The 5 percent who do change their lives hold on to this commitment by working with others to do the same.

What Paul is paying attention to gives an indication of the shift in conversation that might lead to real transformation in the health care industry. The new conversation he is initiating is one of *ownership*. What is our individual and community contribution to the problems we are facing? What *commitment* am I as a citizen willing to make toward my own health? What is the *possibility* of creating wellness in the world rather than fighting disease? What is the *refusal* I am willing to make to the expert and professional control of the conventional solutions? Collaborative rounds is a means for creating a new conversation that places the doctor, the family, the supporting professionals, and the patient all at the center of the planning and decision-making process.

Making these questions central would shift the nature of the health care debate. This conversation would change the context from disease to health, from romance with technology and drugs to actions on the part of the citizen, from discussions of cost control and dependence on the professional to engaging the community. Paul has finally written a book about his work. Read it and join his network.

Example: Dorothy Shaffer

Here's one more example of how transformation happens small, quietly, in rooms designed for humans and based on relatedness. Dorothy Shaffer is a Cincinnati physician in internal medicine. I first noticed she was up to something before I met her. Most mornings I took the kids to school and drove through a neighborhood somewhat on the edge. I noticed on the corner of Reading and Clinton Springs the renovation of an old house that was taking forever. What were they doing there? Why was it taking so long? Strange neighborhood to make that kind of investment . . . Then I forgot about it.

Two years later, I am shopping for a new physician. A friend recommends Dr. Shaffer, who I find out was the one who renovated that building I had been watching. When I go there, I realize she has taken the care to create a version of the possibility of health care. Here is a taste of the future, on the corner of Reading and Clinton Springs.

I call for an appointment, and a human being answers the phone. I ask for an appointment, and she apologizes that I will have to wait three weeks, since I am a new patient. She asks why I want to see the doctor. Tells me that if I become a patient, there will be an annual fee. I agree to this. This is to enable Dr. Shaffer to keep her patient load down to give the service she wants to give. For those who cannot afford the fee, she waives it or figures out what will be possible for that patient.

I show up for my appointment and walk into a living room. It's like staying at a W Hotel, where they redesigned the lobby as a living room. I go to the desk, and on the counter there are raisins, not candy and not nothing. Brenda, the receptionist, who knows me when I call, gives me forms to complete, and when I am done, she says the doctor will be right with me. I sit down and see there are books with some intellectual content: poetry, the environment, nontraditional cures. I have to search hard for *People* and *Time* magazines, both of which are entertaining and content-free. There is no TV on the wall suggesting new treatments.

In four minutes, I am escorted right away to the examining room. The nurse takes my vital signs and weighs me *without* my shoes on. Scale is a little inaccurate on the heavy side, but not to be picky.

Doctor comes in without a clinical coat. Dressed casually in street clothes. We talk, she does the exam, is not anxious about the time. Is interested in my way of eating, my lifestyle, and the stress in my life (takes a while). She knows about vitamin supplements and explains why some are better than others. She thinks part of her job is to educate me.

She is more interested in the person than disease. Most of her focus is on keeping me healthy. Exercise and diet are major focuses for her. Everyone's body resists certain foods, and she suggests we find out about mine. Her office offers acupuncture, massage, and other healing arts, all in the same building. She has organized her service around the patient. I now have one physician who sees the whole picture, one place that treats the whole person.

Dr. Shaffer has eliminated the distinction between conventional and alternative medicine. She has put the patient at the center of the service. She has transformed health care.

If there are people like Paul Uhlig and Dotty Shaffer in one community, then we know there are others like them in all communities. All we have to do is recognize them, support them, and declare them to be mainstream.

I give these two examples for two reasons. First because they embody the idea that communal transformation begins at a small scale, takes a long time, and does not require large funding or a driving concern for efficiency. This means that each of us can join in moving things forward. If we seek large-scale change, we will create it by aggregating a large number of very local efforts like these and finding a way, conceptually, to thread them together under an inclusive umbrella. When a myriad of small efforts to heal the planet got named and woven into an environmental movement, something more impactful was unleashed. Same with the civil rights movement. Decades of local struggles were finally ignited by a few people sitting at a lunch counter and a woman sitting at the front of a bus.

The efforts to transform our communities will be ignited at some point into a movement and a larger commitment to create this world that works for all. It will likely occur when there is some event to bring together our efforts to (1) construct an alternative economy, (2) bring the faith community out of the buildings and into the neighborhoods, (3) stem the tide of privatization and return to giving priority to the common good, and finally (4) declare—and really mean it—that businesses have a much larger purpose than profit.

The second reason to end with the stories of collaborative care and a private medical practice is that the way they function demonstrates the shift in context that this book describes. They operate as if every player in the setting is a cocreator of outcomes. That each patient and patient's family are enough. That they have it within their means to produce health, and that the professional service provider exists to support health, not capitalize on disease.

Also, the way Paul and Dotty (Dr. Shaffer) have constructed their practice has been produced from the thinking that is embodied in the six conversations outlined in the second half of this book. To invent collaborative care, Paul had to choose possibility over problem solving. He had to create space for dissent and the expression of concerns from all parties. He had to broaden the question of commitment to include both the professionals and the patient and family.

Similarly, Dotty created a space that is inviting and welcoming. She creates the possibility that the patient is truly at the center of the conversation. One example of this is in the decision to make the waiting time of the patient as important as the operational efficiency of the doctor. She also demands commitment on the part of the patient. That the patient pays an annual fee to be part of the practice asks for a unique level of commitment. It says that both parties are invested in the fortunes of the practice as well as the fortunes of the patient. To avoid this being elitist, there are ample mechanisms for people with fewer economic resources to be members.

Final point: Community and belonging are a combination of context and initiating a transforming conversation. Shifting our thinking about both the context and the conversation can occur in an instant. In both cases, it is a simple choice. Bringing changes in context and conversation into the world is more complicated. I hope that this book contributes in a small way to moving your efforts forward.

The Social Architecture of Building Community

Building community and belonging in a dominant culture that is based on individualism, competition, and autonomy is difficult work. This section is an attempt to make this easier. It is a quick summary and reference guide to the book. You are welcome to copy and use it at will. First comes the context and main ideas. Next is a summary of the questions. Finally there is a quick look at designing the physical space. Each of these elements is critical.

The core idea is that without a shift in trust, social capital, belonging, relatedness—call it what you wish—our capacity to solve problems, organize work effectively, or end the suffering around us is greatly diminished. Our efforts to discover and implement new programs, pilots, and social innovations will make little difference in a context of scarcity and wide relational disparities. This is true regardless of loving and charitable instincts.

A shift in social capital occurs when we decide that the real transformation is having citizens—strangers up to now—sitting in circles, learning to trust each other, and deciding how to make a place better. To support you in this effort, I have extracted a string of sentences that I think capture its essence, in hopes that some of them will inspire your work to create a world of your own choosing.

Overall Premise

Build social capital by converting the isolation within our communities into connectedness and caring for the whole.

Shift our conversations from the problems of community to the possibility of community.

Bring together people not used to being together into conversations they are not used to having.

Commit to creating a future distinct from the past. One that cares for common good.

Operating Guidelines

Social capital is created one room at a time, the one we are in at the moment.

It is formed out of the questions "Whom do we want in the room?" and "What is the new conversation that we want to occur?"

The key to a new future is to focus on gifts, on associational life, and on the insight that all transformation occurs through language.

Each step has to embody a quality of aliveness, and strategy evolves in an organic way.

The essence of creating an alternative future comes from citizen-to-citizen engagement that constantly focuses on the well-being of the whole.

We have all the capacity, expertise, and financial resources that an alternative future requires.

The small group is the unit of transformation and the container for the experience of belonging.

The Context for a Restorative Community

The existing community context is one that markets fear, assigns fault, and worships self-interest.

This context supports the belief that the future will be improved with new laws, more oversight, and stronger leadership.

The new context, the context that restores community, is one of possibility, generosity, and gifts, rather than one of fear, mistakes, and more problem solving.

Communities are human systems given form by conversations that build relatedness.

The conversations that build relatedness most often occur through associational life, where citizens are unpaid and show up by choice, rather than in large systems where professionals are paid and show up by contractual agreement.

The future hinges on the accountability that citizens choose and their willingness to connect with each other around promises they make to each other.

Citizens have the capacity to own and exercise power rather than defer or delegate it to others.

The Inversion of Cause and Accountability

We reclaim our citizenship when we invert what is cause and what is effect.

Citizens create leaders, children create parents, and the audience creates the performance. This inversion may not be the whole truth, but it is useful.

The inversion creates conditions in which we can shift from a place of fear and fault to one of gifts, generosity, and commitment.

We shift from a bet on law and oversight to one on social capital and chosen accountability, from retributive to restorative justice, from the corporation and systems as central to associational life as central.

We shift from a focus on leaders to a focus on citizens, from a focus on problems to one of possibility.

Leadership and Transformation

Leadership that engages citizens is a capacity that exists in all human beings. It is infinitely and universally available.

Transformation occurs when leaders focus on the structure of how we gather and the context in which the gatherings take place.

Leadership is convening and held to three tasks:

> Shift the context within which people gather.
>
> Name the debate through powerful questions.
>
> Listen rather than advocate, defend, or provide answers.

The Power of the Small Group

Each gathering needs to become an example of the future we want to create.

The small group is the unit of transformation.

Large-scale transformation occurs when enough small groups shift in harmony toward the larger change.

Small groups have the most leverage when they meet as part of a larger gathering.

The small group produces power when diversity of thinking and dissent are given space, commitments are made without barter, and the gifts of each person and our community are acknowledged and valued.

Questions Are More Transforming Than Answers

The skill is getting the questions right.

The traditional conversations that seek to explain, study, analyze, define tools, and express the desire to change others are interesting but not powerful.

Questions open the door to the future and are more powerful than answers in that they demand engagement. Engagement in the right questions is what creates accountability.

How we frame the questions is decisive. They need to be ambiguous, personal, and stressful.

Introduce the questions by defining the distinction the question addresses—namely, what is different and unique about this conversation.

We need to inoculate people against advice and help. Advice is replaced by curiosity.

The Invitation

Invite people who are not used to being together.

The elements of a powerful invitation:

> Name the possibility about which we are convening.
>
> Specify what is required of each citizen should they choose to attend.
>
> Make the invitation as personal as possible.
>
> Be clear that a refusal carries no cost.

The Questions

The five conversations for structuring belonging are possibility, ownership, dissent, commitment, and gifts.

Since all the conversations lead to the others, sequence is not that critical.

Create conversations in ascending order of difficulty, with possibility generally an early conversation and gifts typically one of the more difficult.

There are three elements of a question:

> The distinction that underlies the question
>
> An admonition against advice and help and in favor of curiosity
>
> The question itself, stated precisely

The Possibility Conversation

The distinction is between possibility and problem solving. Possibility is a future beyond reach.

The possibility conversation works on us and evolves from a discussion of personal crossroads. It takes the form of a declaration, best made publicly.

The Questions

What are the crossroads you are faced with at this point in time?

What declaration of possibility can you make that has the power to transform the community and inspire you?

The Ownership Conversation

It asks citizens to act as if they are creating what exists in the world.

The distinction is between ownership and blame. Ownership is the decision to acknowledge our guilt.

The Questions

For an event or project:

How valuable an experience (or project or community) do you plan for this to be?

How much risk are you willing to take?

How participative do you plan to be?

To what extent are you invested in the well-being of the whole?

The all-purpose ownership question:

What have I done to contribute to the very thing I complain about or want to change?

The questions that can complete our story and remove its limiting quality:

What is the story about this community or organization that you hear yourself most often telling? The one you are wedded to and maybe even take your identity from?

What are the payoffs you receive from holding on to this story?

What is your attachment to this story costing you?

The Dissent Conversation

The dissent conversation creates an opening for commitment.

When dissent is expressed, just listen. Don't solve it, defend against it, or explain anything.

The primary distinction is between dissent and lip service.

A second distinction is between dissent and denial, rebellion, or resignation.

The Questions

What doubts and reservations do you have?

What is the no, or refusal, that you keep postponing?

What have you said yes to that you no longer really mean?

What is a commitment or decision that you have changed your mind about?

What forgiveness are you withholding?

What resentment do you hold that no one knows about?

The Commitment Conversation

The commitment conversation is a promise with no expectation of return.

Commitment is distinguished from barter.

The enemy of commitment is lip service, not dissent or opposition.

The commitments that count the most are ones made to peers, other citizens.

We have to explicitly provide support for citizens to declare that there is no promise they are willing to make at this time.

Refusal to promise does not cost us our membership or seat at the table. We only lose our seat when we do not honor our word.

Commitment embraces two kinds of promises:

- Promises about my behavior and actions with others
- Promises about results and outcomes that occur in the world

To pass and make no commitment carries no cost or loss of membership.

The Questions

What promises am I willing to make?

What measures have meaning to me?

What price am I willing to pay?

What is the cost to others for me to keep my commitments, or to fail in my commitments?

What is the promise I'm willing to make that constitutes a risk or major shift for me?

What is the promise I am postponing?

What is the promise or commitment I am unwilling to make?

The Gifts Conversation

The leadership and citizen task is to bring the gifts of those on the margin into the center.

The distinction is between gifts and deficiencies or needs.

We are not defined by deficiencies or what is missing. We are defined by our gifts and what is present.

We choose our destiny when we have the courage to acknowledge our own gifts and choose to bring them into the world. It is the conversion of fate into destiny.

A gift is not a gift until it is offered.

The Questions

What is the gift you currently hold in exile?

What is it about you that no one knows about?

What are you grateful for that has gone unspoken?

What is the positive feedback you receive that still surprises you?

What is the gift you have that you do not fully acknowledge?

What gift have you received from another in this room?

What has someone in your small group done today that has touched you or moved you or been of value to you?

or

In what way did a particular person engage you in a way that had meaning?

What have others in this room done, in this gathering, that has touched you?

The Heart of the Six Conversations

The heart of the conversations emerging from all of these questions is to create a sense of belonging with others and also a sense of accountability for oneself and care for the commons. Here is a summary of the core questions associated with each conversation:

What is the choice you made by being here? (Invitation)

How much risk do you plan to take, and how participative do you plan to be in this gathering or project? (Ownership)

What are the crossroads you/we are at that are appropriate to the purpose of the gathering? (Possibilities)

What declarations are you prepared to make about the possibilities for the future? (Possibilities)

To what extent do you see yourself as cause of the problem you are trying to fix? (Ownership)

What is the story you hold about this community or this issue, and what are the payoffs and costs of this story? (Ownership)

What are your doubts and reservations? (Dissent)

What is the yes you no longer mean? (Dissent)

What promises are you willing to make to your peers? (Commitment)

What gifts have you received from each other? (Gifts)

The important thing about these questions for the possibility, ownership, dissent, commitment, and gifts conversations is that they name the agenda that creates space for an alternative future. The power is in the asking, not in the answers.

Space That Supports Belonging

Physical space is more decisive in creating community than we realize.

Most meeting spaces are designed for control, negotiation, and persuasion.

We always have a choice about how we rearrange and occupy whatever room we are handed.

Community is built when we sit in circles, when there are windows and the walls have signs of life, when every voice can be equally heard and amplified, when we all are on one level—and the chairs have wheels and swivel.

When we have an opportunity to design new space, we need the following:

Reception areas that tell us we are in the right place and are welcome

Hallways wide enough for intimate seating and casual contact

Eating spaces that refresh us and encourage relatedness

Rooms designed with nature, art, conviviality, and citizen-to-citizen interaction in mind

Large community spaces that have the qualities of communal intimacy

The design process itself needs to be an example of the future we are intending to create.

Authentic citizen and employee engagement is as important as good design expertise.

Role Models and Resources

We all need examples of where community is being created. Many of the people and institutions that I am familiar with were listed in the original edition of this book. Rather than including the list in this printing, I have chosen to place it on the Abundant Community website (abundantcommunity.com). There you will find citizens who are bringing the structures of belonging into their communities. This is simply a small personal listing of what actually are tens of thousands of people who build community, not just because it is their job but because of who they are. Please go to the Abundant Community website to see these many examples. And continue to build your own network of local people changing the world.

Background Reading and References

Here is a short list of people and writings that have created the ideas in this book. Authors whom I have quoted directly are also cited here.

Alexander, Christopher

The Nature of Order: An Essay on the Art of Building and the Nature of the Universe, Book 1: The Phenomenon of Life. Berkeley, CA: Center for Environmental Structure, 2002. (Passages quoted in chapter 1 are from pp. 20 and 122.)

The Nature of Order: An Essay on the Art of Building and the Nature of the Universe, Book 2: The Process of Creating Life. Berkeley, CA: Center for Environmental Structure, 2006.

The Nature of Order: An Essay on the Art of Building and the Nature of the Universe, Book 3: A Vision of a Living World. Berkeley, CA: Center for Environmental Structure, 2004.

The Nature of Order: An Essay on the Art of Building and the Nature of the Universe, Book 4: The Luminous Ground. Berkeley, CA: Center for Environmental Structure, 2003.

The Timeless Way of Building. New York: Oxford University Press, 1979.

Axelrod, Dick and Emily

The Conference Model. San Francisco: Berrett-Koehler, 2000.

Terms of Engagement: Changing the Way We Change Organizations. 2nd ed. San Francisco: Berrett-Koehler, 2010.

You Don't Have to Do It Alone: How to Involve Others to Get Things Done. San Francisco: Berrett-Koehler, 2004.

Bornstein, David

How to Change the World: Social Entrepreneurs and the Power of New Ideas. Updated ed. New York: Oxford University Press, 2007.

The Price of a Dream: The Story of the Grameen Bank. Paper reissue. New York: Oxford University Press, 2005.

Brown, Juanita, and David Isaacs

The World Café: Shaping Our Futures Through Conversations That Matter, with the World Café Community. San Francisco: Berrett-Koehler, 2005.

Bunker, Barbara, and Billie T. Alban

The Handbook of Large Group Methods: Creating Systemic Change in Organizations and Communities. San Francisco: Jossey-Bass, 2006.

Large Group Interventions: Engaging the Whole System for Rapid Change. San Francisco: Jossey-Bass, 1997.

Clingman, James

Black Dollars Matter: Teach Your Dollars How to Make Sense. Los Angeles: Professional Publishing House, 2015.

Blackonomic$: The Way to Psychological and Economic Freedom for African Americans. Los Angeles: Milligan Books, 2001.

Dannemiller, Kathie

Whole-Scale Change: Unleashing the Magic in Organizations. San Francisco: Berrett-Koehler, 2000.

Erhard, Werner

Erhard, Werner, Michael C. Jensen, and Steve Zaffron. "Integrity: Where Leadership Begins—A New Model of Integrity (PDF File of PowerPoint Slides)" (June 18, 2007). Barbados Group Working Paper No. 07-03. Available at SSRN: http://ssrn.com/abstract=983401.

Erhard, Werner, Michael C. Jensen, and Steve Zaffron. "A New Model of Integrity: An Actionable Pathway to Trust, Productivity and Value (PDF File of Keynote Slides)" (September 20, 2008). Barbados Group Working Paper No. 07-01. Available at SSRN: http://ssrn.com/abstract=932255.

Gallwey, Tim

The Inner Game of Work: Focus, Learning, Pleasure, and Mobility in the Workplace. Reprint ed. New York: Random House, 2001.

Heschel, Abraham Joshua

Quoted in *I Asked for Wonder: A Spiritual Anthology,* edited by Samuel H. Dresner (New York: Crossroad Publishing, 1983). (See part 1 introduction for quoted passage.)

Jacobs, Jane

Dark Age Ahead. New York: Random House, 2004.

The Death and Life of Great American Cities. 50th anniv. ed. New York: Vintage, 2011. Originally published 1961.

Kahane, Adam

Collaborating with the Enemy: How to Work with People You Don't Agree with or Like or Trust. San Francisco: Berrett-Koehler, 2017.

Solving Tough Problems: An Open Way of Talking, Listening, and Creating New Realities. San Francisco: Berrett-Koehler, 2004.

Kaufman, Harriet

Judaism and Social Justice, by Harriet Kaufman. Personal communication to author, 1986. (Passage quoted in chapter 12 is from Shabbat 77b, Babylonian Talmud.)

Koestenbaum, Peter

Freedom and Accountability at Work: Applying Philosophic Insight to the Real World. San Francisco: Jossey-Bass, 2001.

The Heart of Business: Ethics, Power, and Philosophy. Dallas, TX: Saybrook, 1987.

Leadership: The Inner Side of Greatness. 2nd ed. San Francisco: Jossey-Bass, 2002.

The Philosophic Consultant: Revolutionizing Organizations with Ideas. San Francisco: Jossey-Bass, 2003.

Korten, David

Change the Story, Change the Future: A Living Economy for a Living Earth. San Francisco: Berrett-Koehler, 2015.

The Great Turning: From Empire to Earth Community. San Francisco: Berrett-Koehler, 2006.

When Corporations Rule the World. 2nd ed. San Francisco: Berrett-Koehler, 2001.

Lopez, Barry

Home Ground: Language for an American Landscape, edited by Barry Lopez and Debra Gwartney, with an introduction by Barry Lopez. San Antonio, TX: Trinity University Press, 2006.

McKnight, John

The Abundant Community: Awakening the Power of Families and Neighbor-hoods, with Peter Block. San Francisco: Berrett-Koehler, 2010.

An Other Kingdom: Departing the Consumer Culture, with Walter Brueggemann and Peter Block. Hoboken, NJ: Wiley, 2016.

Building Communities from the Inside Out, with John Kretzmann. Center for Urban Affairs, Evanston, IL. Chicago: ACTA Publications, 1994.

The Careless Society: Community and Its Counterfeits. New York: Basic Books, 1995.

Discovering Community Power: A Guide to Mobilizing Local Assets and Your Organization's Capacity, with John Kretzmann. Chicago: ACTA Publications, 2005.

Mapping Community Capacity, with John Kretzmann. Evanston, IL: Center for Urban Affairs and Policy Research, Northwestern University, 1990.

Neal, Craig and Patricia

The Art of Convening: Authentic Engagement in Meetings, Gatherings, and Conversations, with Cynthia Ward. San Francisco: Berrett-Koehler, 2011.

Owen, Harrison

Open Space Technology: A User's Guide. 3rd ed. San Francisco: Berrett-Koehler, 2008.

The Power of Spirit: How Organizations Transform. San Francisco: Berrett-Koehler, 2000.

The Practice of Peace. 2nd ed. Circle Pines, MN: Human Systems Dynamics Institute, 2004.

Putnam, Robert D.

Better Together: Restoring the American Community, with Lewis M. Feldstein. New York: Simon & Schuster, 2003. (Passages quoted in chapter 1 are from pp. 2–3.)

Bowling Alone: The Collapse and Revival of American Community. New York: Simon & Schuster, 2000.

Rogers, Carl

On Becoming a Person: A Therapist's View of Psychotherapy. 2nd ed. Boston: Mariner Books/Houghton Mifflin Harcourt, 1995. Originally published 1961.

Snow, Judith

What's Really Worth Doing and How to Do It: A Book for People Who Love Someone Labeled Disabled. Toronto, ON: Inclusion Press International, n.d.

The Structurist

University of Saskatchewan. (Passage quoted in Welcome is from no. 45/46, 2005/2006, p. 2.)

Uhlig, Paul

Field Guide to Collaborative Care: Implementing the Future of Health Care, with W. Ellem Raboin. Overland Park, KS: Oak Prairie Health Press, 2015.

"Improving Patient Care in Hospitals," *Journal of Innovative Management*, Goal/QPC, Fall 2001.

"System Innovation: Concord Hospital," with others, *Journal on Quality Improvement*, November 2002.

Weisbord, Marvin

Discovering Common Ground, with 35 International Authors. San Francisco: Berrett-Koehler, 1992.

Don't Just Do Something, Stand There!, with Sandra Janoff. San Francisco: Berrett-Koehler, 2007.

Future Search: An Action Guide to Finding Common Ground in Organizations and Communities, with Sandra Janoff. 3rd ed. San Francisco: Berrett-Koehler, 2010.

Lead More, Control Less: 8 Advanced Leadership Skills That Overturn Convention. Oakland, CA: Berrett-Koehler, 2015.

Productive Workplaces: Organizing and Managing for Dignity, Meaning, and Community. San Francisco: Jossey-Bass, 1987.

Productive Workplaces Revisited: Dignity, Meaning, and Community in the 21st Century. San Francisco: Jossey-Bass/Wiley, 2004.

Zakaria, Fareed

The Future of Freedom: Illiberal Democracy at Home and Abroad. New York: Norton, 2003.

Acknowledgments

Bob Havlick, then head of the Innovation Group, a forward-thinking association of city managers, got me involved in communities. He kept inviting me to their annual conference, and my contact with these public servants shifted the direction of my work. I will always be grateful for Bob's faith and support. Work with some of those city managers—Jim Keene, Jim Ley, Ray Patchett, and Ed Everett—sealed the deal, and I am grateful to all of them.

My gratitude to Peter Koestenbaum, John McKnight, and Werner Erhard is infinite. I keep looking for sentences I speak or write that have not been shaped by their friendship, and I can find few. I do not know whether I have a thought that is truly my own, so I am happily relegated to the role of translator and secondary source for their insights.

Others who have given support to these ideas are Tom DiBello and Jim Tucker. They have invited me into places that were challenging and confirming, so I thank them both.

Bernard Booms thought he was the beneficiary of my work, but the opposite is true. Bernard taught me generosity with each call. Plus he was an economist and a marketing professor who both sustained and transcended his training to bring humanity and care into his work. Special and rare. Passed but not forgotten.

There are certain friends who are constant and always interested. Michael Johnston was an expert on living with integrity, playful when not working, and the best coach on the planet. This sentence sits quietly in his memory.

Leslie Stephen has been my editor for all of the books I have written. She is a beautiful advocate for the reader, has a genius for structure, and is profoundly interested in ideas and how they change the world. Above all, she cares about keeping my voice intact, as ungrammatical as it is. I would stop writing if Leslie were not in the picture. A special thanks for the care given to this second edition.

Steve Piersanti is a dream of a publisher. He has created an independent publishing company that lives out the ideas contained in what he publishes. Steve is a person of enduring faith and has the gift of editing that I pay attention to, even when I am not listening.

The original edition of this book was given life by its reviewers. I want to thank Frank Basler, Jeff Kulick, Ann Matranga, Elianne Obadia, and Joseph A. Webb, for they each put energy, far beyond any compensation for the task, into understanding and caring about the quality of the book. I am also grateful to Elissa Rabellino, who performed the copyediting for the first edition. She gave great attention to the manuscript and was a fine advocate for the reader. Elissa is really good at what she does. Also appreciate the keen eye of Michele Jones in the copyediting of this book.

Thanks also to Cliff Bolster and Bill Brewer, who read an early manuscript and were generous with their thoughts. Allan Cohen and Ann Overton have been central to the ideas in this book. Their friendship is sustaining, and their way of thinking and being is so convergent with mine that when I am in a difficult situation, I often think that they would do a better job than I.

I have dedicated both editions of this book to Maggie Rogers, but to fully acknowledge what she has given to the creation of them and all else I do would require a separate book in itself. Enough here to say thank you again. Years later, at the time of this edition, what I said then is even more so. We have worked together for twenty years at this rewriting, which speaks to her infinite capacity for tolerance.

I also want to express gratitude to my family. Thanks to Jim, my brother, a kind soul who has generously offered his genius as a photographer to all of us; he deserves special thanks for enduring me as a subject. He offered to airbrush my last photo, and next time I will take him up on it. My daughters, Jennifer and Heather, who, through their love, have given me a reason to live a decent life. My grandchildren, Leyland, Gracie, and Auggie, are beautiful beyond the natural pride of a grandfather. They give me reason to live a long time. Finally, I want to express my love for Cathy, David, and Ellen. Every day they keep me on my toes and engaged in a future. With them I am learning the value of surrender, of acceptance, and about the soft and tender fabric that lies within all of us. In return, they put up with me, so who could ask for anything more?

Index

About the Author

Peter Block is an author and citizen of Cincinnati, Ohio. His work is about empowerment, stewardship, chosen accountability, and the reconciliation of community. In his work as a citizen of Cincinnati, he is on a neighborhood council, helped start the Economics of Compassion Initiative, and is mostly working with the concepts of Jubilee, an Old Testament idea awaiting implementation, about forgiving the debts of the poor and returning the land to its rightful owners.

Peter is the author of several best-selling books. The most widely known are *Flawless Consulting: A Guide to Getting Your Expertise Used*, 3rd ed. (Pfeiffer, 2011); *Stewardship: Choosing Service Over Self-Interest*, 2nd ed. (Berrett-Koehler, 2013), and *The Empowered Manager: Positive Political Skills at Work*, 2nd ed. (Wiley, 2016).

He has also authored *The Flawless Consulting Fieldbook and Companion: A Guide to Understanding Your Expertise* (Pfeiffer, 2000), assisted by Andrea Markowitz, and *The Answer to How Is Yes: Acting on What Matters* (Berrett-Koehler, 2002), which won the 2002 Independent Publisher Book Award for Business Breakthrough Book of the Year. *Freedom and Accountability at Work: Applying Philosophic Insight to the Real World* was coauthored with consultant and philosopher Peter Koestenbaum (Jossey-Bass/ Pfeiffer, 2001).

In collaboration with John McKnight, Peter wrote *The Abundant Community: Awakening the Power of Families and Neighborhoods* (Berrett-Koehler, 2010). It is a testimony to John's influence and compassion in the community world. John was trained as an orator, not a writer, so all the ideas in this book derive from John. Peter, in this case, is really a ghostwriter who made it to the title page.

In 2011, Peter and John were "discovered" by Walter Brueggemann, internationally known Old Testament scholar and guiding light in the faith community. Out of their friendship and old-white-men conversations, a book emerged titled *An Other Kingdom: Departing the Consumer Culture* (Wiley, 2016). It is a portal into the intersection of faith and economics.

Peter is also a partner in Designed Learning, a training company he founded that offers workshops that build on the skills outlined in his books. If you would like to learn more about these workshops, contact Designed Learning at 513-524-2227 or visit www.designedlearning.com.

Most relevant to this book, Peter founded A Small Group. Its purpose is to change the dominant narrative of an urban city, Cincinnati in this case, using the six conversations from this book. Elaine and Eric Hansen keep the group going, more than ten years into it. It offers monthly meetings and all-day intensives three times a year in Cincinnati. It also offers online meetings, all of which deepen the conversations in this book. Come if you can.

Peter no longer has an office, but meets people at Lydia's Café in the Clifton neighborhood in Cincinnati. You can visit his websites: www.peter block.com, www.designedlearning.com, www.asmallgroup.net, www .abundantcommunity.com, and www.restore-commons.com. And he welcomes being contacted at pbi@att.net.

About the Design

I believe that the design and feel of a book is as important as its content. There are too many books where I have had to fight the type and interior design in order to extract the content. Small type, crowded pages, no white space, invasive footnotes, no transitions or breathing spaces. These visual qualities in a book neglect the experience of the reader. As if the reader was not important, only the ideas. Leigh McLellan has given her life and talent to book design. She has created a very elegant form for this book and I invited her to comment on the thinking behind her creation:

> The title of the book, *Community: The Structure of Belonging*, suggests both structure and accessibility, a concept enhanced by Peter's open, conversational style. Also, Peter was concerned with judicious use of white space in the design.
>
> The feeling of structure is expressed by the rules (horizontal lines) placed on the part and chapter openings, giving shape to the beginning of each section. On the chapter opening pages, I indented the first lines of the introductory paragraphs to give the reader a little door of white space into the text, an invitation to enter. This indent also creates a more open, informal appearance. To further this and to lend a touch of elegance, I also added space between the letters in the titles and headings.
>
> Quotes are contained in boxes at the edge of the text to lend interest to the page and to give the eye an occasional rest. They also pull the eye outward, momentarily expanding the reading area.
>
> For the text type, I chose a crisp, contemporary face, aptly named Utopia. I complimented the squarishness of the letter shapes with

Tiepolo Bold for the titles, and selected sans serif Frutiger for contrast in handling the different kinds of text in the book, especially the introductory paragraph and the Example text. The title and halftitle pages are set with Frutiger capitals as a lead-in from the san serif cover type. The large dot on both pages reflects the circular cover motif.

Book design in sum: structure, elegance, consistency, an organic whole in which every part pulls and pushes every other part with both tension and harmony. Each element must be distinct yet recognizably related. Interconnected, like members of a community, as Peter so beautifully expressed in his Welcome.

—*Leigh McLellan*

www.abundantcommunity.com

Visit the website developed by Peter Block and John McKnight to showcase the work featured in their book *The Abundant Community: Awakening the Power of Families and Neighborhoods.*

- Discover the methods that community-minded people around the world use to discover new ways to cooperate in fulfilling the productive functions of communities.

- Learn the latest thinking about what it means to live in an Abundant Community.

- Read blog posts contributed by social innovators who are changing the narrative about their community.

- Listen to Peter and John talk with people who are creating the kind of community that has the power to reweave the social fabric undone by our consumerist culture.

- Watch videos of examples of people and neighborhoods that have found practical ways to use local gifts and talents to create a future that works for all.

NEW!
Community Role Models and Resources

To mark the publication of the second edition of *Community: The Structure of Belonging,* The Abundant Community website now features a completely updated Role Models and Resources list from Peter's book, newly designed for easy access and regular updating.

Share your neighborhood's story at **www.abundantcommunity.com** and sign up for The Abundant Community newsletter announcing the periodic online / dial-up conversations Peter and John have with community-building pioneers from across the country and around the world.

www.restore-commons.com

Citizen-leaders are inventing ways for themselves and their neighbors to be safe, produce a just economy, produce good health, produce and distribute a secure and local food supply, care for people on the margin, care for the land, and do a better job of raising our children. These are the measures of care for the common good.

Building the social fabric of our culture required to support the commons is a long-term undertaking. It starts with seeing the nature of the modern epidemic of isolation and then constructing ways of reversing it. There is a need to shift the thinking, narratives, and practices that produce this isolation.

An initiative of Peter Block and friends, Restore Commons aims to assemble the principles, practices, and tools for this restorative transformation, which is well under way.

Restore Commons is designed to be an online gathering place for stories and radical ideas strong enough to build the social capital and engaged community required to restore the common good. The topics include:

- an alternative economy
- alternative journalism
- neighborhoods, architecture, and space that connect us
- voices from the faith community who are reinterpreting text in powerful and surprising ways

Visit the website to find examples and discover thought leaders sharing inverted and humanistic thinking through videos, podcasts, stories, and recommended reading.

Stay connected!

- Sign up for the free newsletter at **www.restore-commons.com**
- Engage on **Facebook** and **Twitter**: @RestoreCommons

a Peter Block company

Peter Block's Designed Learning continues to lead the industry in providing workplace business partnering, leadership, and consulting skills training. At the center of the world of organizational change for over 30 years, Designed Learning has trained over 1,000,000 people in hundreds of companies worldwide using Peter Block's Flawless Consulting® workshops.

Based on Peter's best-selling *Flawless Consulting: A Guide to Getting Your Expertise Used*, these highly interactive workshops teach participants the skills that will allow them to effectively partner with peers and those above them in order to have their expertise used and recommendations implemented even in situations where they have little or no control. The workshops teach personally powerful ways to be more authentic, express wants, give support, disarm objections, and be more confident in partnership roles, both professionally and personally.

We want to have a conversation with you. Give us a call or visit our website at **www.designedlearning** to learn more about Designed Learning and Flawless Consulting workshops, the only workshops designed and continually developed by Peter Block.

Phone: 513-524-2227 or 1-866-770-2227 (Toll-free)
Email: administrator@designedLearning.com

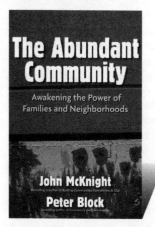

Also by Peter Block

Stewardship
Choosing Service over Self-Interest, Second Edition

Stewardship remains as relevant and radical today as when it was first published in 1993. Block asserts that a fundamental shift in how we distribute power, privilege, and the control of money can transform every part of an organization for the better. This edition features a new introduction by Block and a new chapter on applying stewardship to the common good of the wider community.

Paperback, 312 pages, ISBN 978-1-60994-822-1
PDF ebook, ISBN 978-1-60994-823-8
ePub ebook ISBN 978-1-60994-824-5

The Answer to How Is Yes
Acting on What Matters

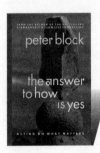

Modern culture's worship of "how-to" pragmatism has turned us into instruments of efficiency and commerce—but we're doing more and more about things that mean less and less. Peter Block raises our awareness of the trade-offs we've made in the name of practicality and offers hope for a way of life in which we're motivated not by what "works" but by things that truly matter—idealism, intimacy, depth, and engagement.

Paperback, 216 pages, ISBN 978-1-57675-271-5
PDF ebook, ISBN 978-1-60509-394-9
ePub ebook ISBN 978-1-60994-040-9

BK Berrett–Koehler Publishers, Inc.
www.bkconnection.com   **800.929.2929**

Berrett–Koehler
BK Publishers

Berrett-Koehler is an independent publisher dedicated to an ambitious mission: *Connecting people and ideas to create a world that works for all.*

We believe that the solutions to the world's problems will come from all of us, working at all levels: in our organizations, in our society, and in our own lives. Our BK Business books help people make their organizations more humane, democratic, diverse, and effective (we don't think there's any contradiction there). Our BK Currents books offer pathways to creating a more just, equitable, and sustainable society. Our BK Life books help people create positive change in their lives and align their personal practices with their aspirations for a better world.

All of our books are designed to bring people seeking positive change together around the ideas that empower them to see and shape the world in a new way.

And we strive to practice what we preach. At the core of our approach is Stewardship, a deep sense of responsibility to administer the company for the benefit of all of our stakeholder groups including authors, customers, employees, investors, service providers, and the communities and environment around us. Everything we do is built around this and our other key values of quality, partnership, inclusion, and sustainability.

This is why we are both a B-Corporation and a California Benefit Corporation—a certification and a for-profit legal status that require us to adhere to the highest standards for corporate, social, and environmental performance.

We are grateful to our readers, authors, and other friends of the company who consider themselves to be part of the BK Community. We hope that you, too, will join us in our mission.

A BK Business Book

We hope you enjoy this BK Business book. BK Business books pioneer new leadership and management practices and socially responsible approaches to business. They are designed to provide you with groundbreaking and practical tools to transform your work and organizations while upholding the triple bottom line of people, planet, and profits. High-five!

To find out more, visit **www.bkconnection.com**.

Berrett–Koehler
Publishers

Connecting people and ideas
to create a world that works for all

Dear Reader,

Thank you for picking up this book and joining our worldwide community of Berrett-Koehler readers. We share ideas that bring positive change into people's lives, organizations, and society.

To welcome you, we'd like to offer you a free e-book. You can pick from among twelve of our bestselling books by entering the promotional code **BKP92E** here: http://www.bkconnection.com/welcome.

When you claim your free e-book, we'll also send you a copy of our e-newsletter, the *BK Communiqué*. Although you're free to unsubscribe, there are many benefits to sticking around. In every issue of our newsletter you'll find

- A free e-book
- Tips from famous authors
- Discounts on spotlight titles
- Hilarious insider publishing news
- A chance to win a prize for answering a riddle

Best of all, our readers tell us, "Your newsletter is the only one I actually read." So claim your gift today, and please stay in touch!

Sincerely,

Charlotte Ashlock
Steward of the BK Website

Questions? Comments? Contact me at bkcommunity@bkpub.com.

Certified

Corporation
bcorporation.net